Forgive and
Be Free

HEALING THE WOUNDS OF
PAST AND PRESENT

Forgive and Be Free

HEALING THE WOUNDS OF PAST AND PRESENT

RICHARD P. WALTERS

PYRANEE
BOOKS

Zondervan Publishing House
Grand Rapids, Michigan

Forgive and Be Free: Healing the Wounds of Past and Present
Copyright © 1983 by The Zondervan Corporation

Pyranee Books are published by Zondervan
Publishing House, 1415 Lake Drive, S.E.,
Grand Rapids, Michigan 49506

Library of Congress Cataloging in Publication Data

Walters, Richard P.
    Forgive and be free.

    1. Forgiveness.   I. Title.
BJ1476.W34   1983   241'.4   82-21848
ISBN 0-310-42611-1

Edited by Julie Ackerman Link
Designed by Louise Bauer

Printed in the United States of America

86 87 88 89 90 / 12 11 10 9 8 7 6 5

Contents

Preface

FORGIVING WORKS MIRACLES. I have seen this time and time again in counseling situations. Forgiving can accomplish what the authors of most counseling and psychotherapy textbooks only dream about accomplishing.

Forgiving has power to heal because it is God's process. We have an essential part in it, but forgiving is not possible without God's help.

Many of us have been taught the importance of forgiving without being instructed in how to forgive. Feelings of guilt or failure and confusion about whether or not one has actually forgiven have often been the result. This book will illustrate how forgiving has changed people's lives and will coach you in the process of forgiving so that you can attain the full measure of joy available to you.

Read this book with anticipation of joy to come, for if you respond to our Lord's prompting and forgive what you have not forgiven, new freedom and peace will be yours. Read with an open mind, hoping to find confrontation in these words that will convict you of forgiving that you need to do. And as you read, pray that God will teach you about the forgiving you need to do; then act on what you learn.

The summary and action plans at the end of the book should be used to help you explore various aspects of problems and various parts of your life. God can speak to you through the Holy Spirit as you use those. Do not think of those materials as formulas for how to do something, but as devices for disciplining your thinking.

God has custom-tailored plans to accomplish the forgiving you need to do. Ask God to show you His plans, to help you understand them, and to help you implement them.

My wish for you is that you would come to experience the most complete kind of living God has for you. The path to a complete relationship with another person always leads through forgiving.

Some of the illustrations are based on actual events, but all characters are fictional. Any similarity to real individuals is coincidental and results only from the fact that we are much more alike than we are different.

A small amount of this material has appeared in *Boldness: The Proactive Lifestyle,* a workbook by Richard P. Walters, published by Christian Helpers, Inc., and is reprinted by permission of the copyright owner.

Thank you, Helen Brinks, for typing mumbled dictation and scribbled revisions; Carol Holquist, Cheryl Forbes, and Julie Ackerman Link of Zondervan Publishing House for encouragement and astute recommendations; Pine Rest Christian Hospital for the opportunity to present workshops on this topic as part of its commitment to help people live in wholeness. And special thanks to those in the forgiving community in which I live, Rachel, Dan, and Amy, who forgive me on occasions—far too frequent—when I fail to live up to what I have written.

Most of all, thank you, Lord, for forgiveness so freely and mercifully given us. Without you we are nothing. Help us each to learn how to humbly live out our opportunities to pass along to others the love you so generously shower on us.

1 | The Terrible Price of Not Forgiving

ALL THAT LAZY KID does is lie around the house all day long. He ought to be out looking for work! He's twenty-three years old, but what does he do? Nothing! He lives like a five-year-old. He wouldn't get out of bed at all if the cartoons didn't come on T.V."

"Don't be so hard on him, John. After all he's been through it's only fair for us to be patient with him."

"Patient?" John exploded. "I put up with him being on drugs, I paid for his treatments, and now it's his turn to do what I tell him to do. Brent has been out and done his thing. Now he has come back, and I have forgiven him. I danced to his tune, and now it's turned around the other way. That's all there is to it."

"John, please don't be harsh on him. He's still a boy emotionally. Just because he has a few faults, just because he doesn't measure up in a few little ways you don't have to be so tough with him."

"I have forgiven him and he should be thankful for that. It's ultimatum time now. Either he starts appreciating all that I have done or it's back on the street."

Brent had made a lot of mistakes. As a human

being, and therefore sinful and rebellious (aren't we all?), he had done things that hurt those who loved him (haven't we all?). He remained unappreciative of the help offered him (don't we all?).

Brent had problems that had to be worked out—he needed to repent and change, he needed to mature. But let's look at the mistakes that his parents, who were both serious about their Christian faith, were making.

FORGIVING WITH STRINGS ATTACHED

John, Brent's father, offered to forgive, but was ready to pull back his forgiving if Brent didn't do what John had decided he should do. It was true that Brent needed a new lifestyle, but John's conditional forgiving kept him in the competitive position with Brent that had made rebelling appeal to Brent in the first place.

Partial forgiving prevented father and son from developing free, full love for one another. It gave Brent excuses for staying in his destructive lifestyle and encouraged John to remain the belligerent critic. Neither of the men was moving toward maturity.

It was a terrible price to pay for half-hearted forgiving.

CHEAP FORGIVING

On the other hand, Muriel, Brent's mother, was ready to forgive anything and everything, no questions asked, and she voiced no expectations for improved behavior. Easy forgiving like this becomes a salve that temporarily relieves the sinner's pain and reduces the motivation to repent before God. Cheap grace is bad enough, but grace offered by those who have no power to remove real guilt is the most worthless of all responses to the problem of sin.

Muriel found it easy to say she was forgiving because she closed her eyes to the seriousness of the problems. This was her way of protecting herself. Her willingness to ignore problems had made it easy for Brent to get into more and more destructive behavior. He squandered five years of his life drifting through the American drug subculture with nothing more to show for it than an intractable venereal disease, residual effects of hepatitis, and deeply embedded aimlessness.

"I'LL FORGIVE THE SMALL STUFF, BUT . . ."

Jack grew up in the shadow of an older brother who was an outstanding athlete, a natural leader, and a strong student who went through graduate school in minimum time. His parents were active in civic affairs, although his mother probably was a do-gooder for selfish reasons. Jack, clumsy and shy, chose to be rebellious in school rather than to be the good student he might have been. He dropped out of high school because it interfered with his drinking and found a job in a factory where alcoholism, obsessive lust, compulsive sex, drug use, and low self-esteem were tolerated, if not fostered.

After eleven years of this unsatisfying life Jack quit drinking, sought help with marital and personal problems, and a couple of years later accepted Christ. The changes in him during this time were astonishing. His self-esteem began to develop, the competitiveness and comparisons with his brother began to diminish, and he began once again to spend time with his parents. He learned to forgive them for little things, such as being critical of his wife or meddling in the discipline of his child; but resentment toward them for the old favoritism toward his older brother continued to burn within him.

Although forgiving the smaller hurts was desirable, it was not enough. Hanging on to old and significant resentment diluted the joy he could have had with his parents. It led to feelings of shame, caused real guilt because of his hard attitude, and marred his fellowship with God.

It was a terrible price to pay for not forgiving.

ABOVE IT ALL

"When he brings me my mother's rocking chair, that's when I'll speak to him again," Elsie said. "Until then, as far as I'm concerned, he doesn't even exist."

When Elsie's mother died, her brother, executor of the estate, sat down to try to figure out how her belongings were going to be divided among five daughters and two sons. He took the quickest way out. He called an antique dealer and sold the furnishings of the family home in one lot. He did it so quickly that Elsie didn't know about it until her brother stopped by to give her a check for her share. She was furious.

She told him off. She yelled. She cried. She swore. And she said she would never speak to him again.

She felt guilty about that almost immediately. As a Christian she knew she needed to apologize to him for her behavior and to forgive him for his impulsive action. But she was too proud.

This was the beginning of a vicious cycle. She discovered that she could numb the guilt by binge eating. But then, because of an extraordinary fear of getting fat and being rejected by her husband, she would cause herself to vomit. This added feelings of shame to her guilt about the way she had treated her brother.

It was a terrible price to pay for not forgiving.

DELIBERATELY BOGUS

Harold's wife had been unfaithful to him. He referred to it so often and seemed to get such delight in telling about it, people got the impression that Harold thought it was the best thing that had ever happened to him.

Soon after the incident of adultery Harold had

prayed aloud in a church group saying, "Thank you, Lord, for helping me to be a forgiving person in this time of awful pain in my life." Even a couple years after it happened he talked about the subject of forgiving whenever he could work it into the conversation, and he always spoke of how much better his own life had been since he had learned to forgive. He always dropped in enough hints to let the listener know what his wife had done.

Meanwhile, he was withholding sex from his wife in a passive-aggressive form of retaliation that strongly suggested he had not forgiven her. The marriage remained substandard in spite of the fact that his wife was genuinely repentant and was pleading with Harold to participate with her in marriage counseling. He remained resentful, and his phony pretenses of spiritual maturity caused additional guilt and burden.

It was a terrible price to pay for not forgiving.

SELF-DELUSION

Eva had been ridiculed by another person in a committee meeting and had retorted with a vicious insult. Later she apologized for her behavior and believed that was the end of the incident. She remained quite distant from that person, however, an indication that she was nursing a grudge. When she would become aware of this resentment, she would push it away from her thinking by reminding herself how good she was for apologizing for her own wrong behavior.

Eva had done a very difficult thing when she apologized, but that had taken care of only part of the problem. Eva needed to forgive the person for the original ridicule as well. But instead she was resentful, not only of the original ridicule, but of the fact that the other person had not apologized.

Eva found herself becoming increasingly more uncomfortable around the other person and eventually withdrew from the committee they had both been on. This was a bad choice not only because it was a way of escaping from the problem rather than dealing directly and appropriately with it, but also because Eva had enjoyed that committee.

It was a terrible price to pay for not forgiving.

BEGRUDGING

The week after the roof leaked and Bill signed a contract for twenty-eight hundred dollars for repairs he felt so gloomy that he bought a three-hundred-dollar tape deck for his car to cheer himself up. He charged it on his credit card, not knowing where the money to pay for it would come from. Beth was angry and worried about the expenses, and thought that Bill had been childish and selfish.

"Be reasonable, can't you?" Bill said. "Give me space to be a little human." He went on to beg and plead for her to let it go saying, "Forgive me, for crying out loud. You're the Christian in the family, and isn't that what you Christians are supposed to be so good at?"

Beth knew that, yes, as a Christian she was supposed to be good at forgiving. So she said, "Well, okay, I forgive you," and pretended that she really had. And she tried to ignore the continuing stress of anger and worry.

But the pretending didn't work. Instead, the anger and worry grew, and the way they handled the tape deck incident became a wedge that slowly, but powerfully, began pushing them apart. And, just as a log-splitting wedge will push the harder with each sledgehammer blow until there is a sudden CRACK! when the log splits, so there was a point in Bill's and Beth's marriage when CRACK!, the bond that had held them together was broken.

It was a terrible price to pay for not forgiving.

UNAWARE

Callie had grown up in a friendly Christian home, but felt she had never gotten any respect. Years ago her father had told her he thought she wasn't cut out for going to high school and asked her to take a job in a factory to help support the family. She did, but she felt rejected by him and felt that she was no good. Over the years this developed into self-imposed demands that she have the cleanest house on the block, the quietest kids in church, and the best-tasting cookies at the socials—basically that she have a nearly perfect performance in every area of life.

In addition, she remained very sensitive to rejection and loneliness. During a time of family stress she stumbled onto a way of getting attention from the family—she began refusing to go shopping by herself. She manipulated family members into going with her. Eventually it came to the point where she was very anxious when she had to go by herself, and she was virtually incapacitated by her anxiety.

Her problems had their roots in the action taken by her father. He had meant well, but he had made a mistake. She had been angry about that for nearly twenty years, but was not aware of that anger.

She did not understand where her problems were coming from, but she knew what it was costing her. She was a slave to her perfectionist standards, living in fear of being outdone by a neighbor or criticized by a family member.

It was a terrible price to pay for not forgiving.

ULTIMATE FRUSTRATION

Each of these persons had been hurt in life by another person or by circumstances. Each person needed to forgive, but had not.

The biggest mistake we can make in life is to reject God's offer to forgive our sins against Him. The second biggest mistake we can make in life is to fail to forgive others who have hurt us.

When we don't forgive, life is like being alone in a deep hole. Our freedom is gone. By day we see the sun overhead, hear the talk and laughter of others as they enjoy life, and know that we are missing out on the joy of living that we should have. By night we sit huddled, lonely and fearful, in the bottom of this pit, angry at ourselves for having dug the pit and for having stepped into it through our failure to forgive.

Resentment begins to control our lives. Forgiving is the only cure for resentment, but pride lies between. Rather than deny/defy our pride, we look for an easy way out. But as we try to climb up the rough, gravelly sides, we slip back as much as we progress. We grow frustrated, panicky.

Perhaps it is like being a tiny insect trapped inside the upper portion of an hourglass. We feel the sand running out beneath us and feel terror in our hearts, knowing that if we don't scramble as fast as we can, non-stop, we will drop right through the bottom and be buried under more sand that will rain down on us from above. It takes every fragment of our energy to stay in one place. We see no way out.

This is the trap we get into when we fail to forgive. Callie discovered, as you will read in the next chapter, that there is a way out.

2 | Callie Escapes From Her Trap

CALLIE, LIVING IN THE top of the hourglass, felt as though she was running as fast as she could and going nowhere. Her life was controlled by the demands she put on herself to be perfect. She was not leaving the house very much because those old feelings of being worthless had grown to such a point that she interpreted even a glance from a stranger in a mall as condemnation. Her life was badly disabled, as commonly happens when resentment is allowed to fester over a period of years.

Callie did not understand where her problems began. She loved her parents and was very happy that her children could live in the same town with their grandparents. Many family and church activities were superficially enjoyable to Callie. But living in the top of the hourglass, she felt the sand skidding from beneath her feet and felt perilously close to dropping into the pit below—"going down the tubes" was the way she expressed it.

Callie began to ask God to teach her the things she needed to learn about her attitudes and her thinking. In response to those prayers she discovered her resentment toward her father. She realized that holding all that resentment within her had been wrong. She confessed it to the Lord, and asked for and received His forgiveness.

She then had a new perspective on what had happened many years before and realized, after talking it out carefully with her husband and with a counselor, that her father's decision had not been a good one and that it had been harmful to her. She forgave her father.

She prayed for guidance about whether or not she should talk with her father about it. She finally concluded that it would not please God for her to bring up the subject because the conversation would hurt her father.

At the point she forgave her father, Callie broke free from the horrible trap of resentment. No longer did she have to prove herself with her vacuum cleaner and her oven. She became free to invite neighbors to her home to get acquainted, to have fun, to serve coffee and cookies to, and to share fellowship.

No longer did she sit in church inwardly trembling with fear that someone might think her children were too noisy. She was free to worship God, to let her joyous heart take flight on wings of praise and soar upward in celebration of God's loving mercy.

No longer did she stay home, angry at herself for being afraid to go shopping alone. She became free not only to go shopping, but to take a job. And within a few months she became manager of a retail store.

This is the only worthwhile kind of forgiving—complete. It is the kind of forgiving God wants us to experience in life; because when we hold back forgiveness, we miss out on the fullness of living and the wholeness and healing that God wants us to have.

What is forgiving? Forgiving is giving up all claim on one who has hurt you and letting go of the emotional consequences of the hurt.

How can we do that? It's done at the price of beating back our pride. By nature we are selfish. Forgiving, by definition, is unselfish. Being hurt by another person wounds our pride. Pride stands in the way of forgiving. We cannot forgive without God's help. It might be possible for us to forgive something inconsequential without God's help; but in significant matters, we are unlikely to accomplish anything without God's involvement in the process.

When do we need to forgive? We need to forgive when we have been hurt by others—whether or not that hurt was intentional and whether or not the person was aware of it. If we do not forgive, we remain bound by resentment, selfishness, rebellion, and other forms of pride.

How does forgiving happen? There is not any set pattern. It is usually a process over a period of time, not something that happens at a particular instant. There often are, however, strategic moments during the process.

This book tells how various individuals dealt with situations in which they needed to forgive. Each chapter will illustrate one or two important truths about the forgiving process. Each person's process of forgiving may include any of these in any combination; no doubt there are many other variations in the process of forgiving. God will lead each of us to the information we need in order to proceed.

What is it worth? Callie said, "My life has changed completely since I learned to forgive. Before, although I had confidence about the next life, this life was miserable. I wasn't living, I was surviving—just barely surviving. Now I wake up in the morning with enthusiasm instead of dread. Our entire family is so much closer than before. Life is in color instead of in black and white! This is the most valuable thing that ever happened in my adult life. It's worth everything. It's infinitely valuable. No, it's better than that!" She radiated joy and confidence as she spoke, "Forgiveness is of infinite value times two!"

3 | Infinite Value Times Two

CALLIE MAY NOT HAVE been mathematically precise when she said that "forgiveness is of infinite value times two," but she understood the important part— the value of forgiveness is beyond our human comprehension. Forgiveness has two directions, and both are of infinite value.

The first direction of forgiveness is vertical: God forgives us for our sins against Him. This is the Good News, the incredible fact that through the life, death, and resurrection of Jesus Christ, we can personally know God and receive His forgiveness of our sins. This is the most powerful force—the only sufficient force—for personal change!

Receiving God's forgiveness frees us from guilt, the fact of our sin, and normally frees us from shame, the unpleasant feeling we have when we are aware of our guilt. It makes clear communication with God possible and enables us to receive His direct support through the Holy Spirit, our comforter and guide.

Salvation, God's forgiveness of our sins, removes the guilt of our past sins. Forgiveness makes it possible for us to grow into personal competence, develop satisfying relationships with others, and enjoy full partnership with God in the adventure of life. It gives opportunity for success and meaning in this life while we are on our way to a perfect life of never-ending joy. Salvation is the most exhilarating message of all history, the most exciting fact in the universe, and surely of infinite value because our response to this message has consequences that will remain throughout eternity.

The second direction of forgiveness is horizontal: we forgive others for their sins against us. This, too, brings tremendous freedom!

When we forgive people who have hurt us, we escape from the top of the hourglass. Forgiving frees us from resentment, from false and unnecessary guilt, and from a thousand forms of bondage in which we trap ourselves. Forgiving has tremendous healing power. It can heal the pain of rejection; it can heal the stress and tensions of conflict; it can heal the disgust we may feel for ourselves; it can heal fear; and it can heal emptiness.

God wants us to live joyously. His plan in sending Christ and the Holy Spirit to minister to us was to free us from the burdens of sin. Jesus said, "I have come that they may have life, and have it to the full" (John 10:10). Accepting this offer begins the process of healing and growth—with eternal consequences for us and for those around us, and surely of infinite value!

We need to forgive because the Bible commands it. Christ's words in Matthew 6:14–15, "For if you forgive men when they sin against you, your heavenly Father will also forgive you. But if you do not forgive men their sins, your Father will not forgive your sins," show the importance of forgiving others, as do the statements about forgiving that are part of the Lord's Prayer (Matt. 6:9–13 and Luke 11:2–4).

Why does God command that we forgive? Because He loves us. This is the only reason God ever commands anything. Therefore, forgiving must be good for us; and it is!

First, it is good for us because it allows us to maintain fellowship with God. This fellowship should be the source of enthusiasm and security in our day-to-day activities; it is the gasoline that runs our engine; the cornerstone on which we build the house of our life. We should follow God's commands out of obedience, but we should understand that all of God's commands are given because He loves us and that every command works to our benefit in this life as well as in the next. Not forgiving others interrupts our fellowship with God (Matt. 5:21–24 and Mark 11:25).

Second, forgiving is important in order to maintain fellowship with others. Paul emphasizes this in Ephesians 4:32 when he writes, "Be kind and compassionate to one another, forgiving each other, just as in Christ God forgave you." That counsel is repeated in Colossians 3:13. "Bear with each other and forgive whatever grievances you may have against one another. Forgive as the Lord forgave you." He describes the integration of love into a lifestyle of servanthood in Romans 12:17–21. "Do not repay anyone evil for evil. Be careful to do what is right in the eyes of everybody. If it is possible, as far as it depends on you, live at peace with everyone. Do not take revenge, my friends, but leave room for God's wrath, for it is written: 'It is mine to avenge; I will repay,' says the Lord."

Third, we need to forgive to avoid the costs of not forgiving. Not forgiving prolongs hurt and anger and leads to smoldering resentment which will make us miserable until it kills us. Resentment destroys the perception of reality. As we try to bend the world to accommodate our resentment, fear, and selfishness, we become less accurate in understanding the world. This eventually destroys our ability to cope successfully with life.

Failure to forgive leads to a judgmental spirit, which is not only unhealthy, but as Luke 6:37–38 states, is also wrong. "Do not judge, and you will not be judged. Do not condemn, and you will not be condemned. Forgive, and you will be forgiven. Give, and it will be given to you. A good measure, pressed down, shaken together and running over, will be poured into your lap. For with the measure you use, it will be measured to you."

How often do we view a situation through the "plank" of our own pride as we attempt to remove the "sawdust speck" from the other person's eye (Matt. 7:1–5)? When we do this, we not only put ourselves in conflict with the other person, but we miss abundant blessings from God. In the parable of the unmerciful servant (Matt. 18:23–35), Jesus contrasts God's generous spirit with the smallness of our human nature. Let's seek to be more like God. Even after forgiving, we will still have the memory of the injustice that was done to us, but it will no longer hurt us.

Even if we could forget, that would be second best because forgetting can only take us back to zero; forgiving, on the other hand, is an opportunity for growth beyond zero. If we could forget, we would not recognize the need to forgive and we would miss out on all the positive effects of forgiving.

Remembering the injustice and our response to it has some benefits. It can help us avoid committing a similar injustice against another; it can help us understand ourselves better; from it we can learn to improve our relationships with others; and, as a result of it, we may be able to teach others about God's healing power.

Best of all, forgiving an injustice is a direct experience in living in partnership with our Lord. It is a reminder of His power within us, which enables us to become overcomers. Hallelujah!

Forgiving often seems so difficult that we are

tempted to try to suppress our feelings and thoughts about the injustice. This is a poor choice. Forgiving is forever, suppressing is not. With suppressing there is always the uneasy specter of remembering. But after forgiving we can relax because we are able to think about the grievance without being jabbed with pain, anger, and the desire for revenge. We choose to not think about it, but we are not encumbered by having to avoid it.

Fourth, forgiving leads to growth and freedom. Resentment destroys relationships; forgiving develops relationships. It helps build a platform of self-worth and confidence on which we can erect a mature life. If love and reassurance were missing from past relationships, God can fill in the emotional empty spots and take away any other obstacles that might prevent us from living fully and freely.

And fifth, forgiving can benefit others. When we forgive a person who has felt guilty about what he has done to us, it releases that person from that feeling. Forgiving others is an example of mature Christian faith in practice.

But forgiving is difficult because it demands unselfishness, and we are selfish by nature. It seems unfair to have to forgive because those who have done wrong do not seem to deserve forgiveness. We look at things through a system of legal justice similar to the Old Testament custom demanding "an eye for an eye." But instead, forgiving is a matter of mercy, as exemplified by Christ's death on the cross that makes it possible for us to receive God's forgiveness.

Because of forgiveness it is possible for us to forgive. I like to use the word *forgiving* to talk about the horizontal aspect of the topic to contrast it with forgiveness from God. When God forgives, it is not a process. God can instantly forgive completely. Only rarely does that happen when we forgive one another. The use of the term *forgiving* helps keep us from becoming complacent and from thinking that we have forgiven completely when we have not.

Forgiving does not mean condoning the wrong the other person has done. The person is still responsible to God for his/her sins. We forgive all who hurt us, as Christ, on the cross, forgave those who in ignorance, disbelief, and rebelliousness sinned against Him (Luke 23:34), but we are obligated to confront our brothers even as we must forgive (Luke 17:3–4).

Forgiving does not change the other person. We may be hurt again in the same way by that person. We should not leave ourselves open to abuse, but it may occur. And if it does, part of our response must be to forgive again.

Forgiving those who have wounded us is required, but it also makes healing possible. It is a process that may take some time, but it is well worth the spiritual and relational discipline that it requires. Forgiving major hurts is possible only with God's help. And fortunately, God wants to help us.

Chapters 5 through 13 tell how several people dealt with situations that called for forgiving. Each chapter will illustrate one or two important points about forgiving. Then, chapters 14 through 17 show how to apply the principles in our own lives. We should approach these principles determined to let God teach us all we need to learn about forgiving. Right now, let's turn to a common bit of bad advice: forgive and forget.

4 | Better Than Forgetting

FORGIVE AND FORGET is a cliché. It's a nice idea, but it doesn't work. It is foolish advice because it is impossible to do. It is impossible to forget something we are trying to forget!

Studies of the way our brains work show that we do not forget anything that has ever been important enough to us to have been stored in our long-term memory. Many stimuli entering our sensory systems (through sight, hearing, smell, touch, taste) do not remain for more than a second or two. Those that remain go into short-term memory where they are "sorted" for their importance to us. The unimportant stimuli are forgotten within fifteen to twenty seconds; the important impressions are transferred to long-term memory. This part of our brain is like a gigantic warehouse full of filing cabinets in which everything that enters remains stored for our lifetime, unless the warehouse is damaged by disease or accident. Scientific studies repeatedly have demonstrated that impressions stored in long-term memory remain there and can be remembered even years and years later. There may be psychological resistance to remembering, an unconscious process called repression, but the memory is there.*

The more important a piece of information is to us, the more quickly we will be able to pull it out of storage in long-term memory, and the more often we will do that. This is particularly true when the information has a strong emotional connection.

When we need to forgive someone it is because they have been unjust to us in some way. Injustice that happens to others can be ignored, but when it happens to us it nearly always triggers strong emotional responses. The incident and our response to it go into long-term memory, and, unless we do something to settle the emotional unrest, we will frequently review the memory and begin to have all the complications that resentment leads to.

We must know that God has forgiven our sins, but I expect that we will always remember our past sins. God remembers them, too. If, when God forgave us, He forgot about them and we still remembered them, that would make us, in that one small way, more knowledgeable than God, which we can never be. All knowledge—past, present, future—exists with God at this moment, as it always has and always will.

God does something better than forget: He forgives. With forgiveness the knowledge of the sin remains, but it no longer matters. God's style of forgiving is clearly shown in Micah 7:18–19. "Who is a God like you, who pardons sin and forgives the transgression? . . . You do not stay angry forever but delight to show mercy. You will again have compassion on us; you will tread our sins underfoot and hurl all our iniquities into the depths of the sea." Forgiven incidents are no longer important. This is God's style, and He wants it to be our style, too.

---

*For reviews of the literature on memory, consult: Loftus, E.F. *Memory.* Reading, MA: Addison-Wesley Publishing Co., Inc. 1980. Neisser, U. (Ed.) *Memory Observed: Remembering in Natural Contexts.* San Francisco: W. H. Freeman and Co. 1982.

Forgiving is a realistic objective. Unfortunately, many people take on themselves the impossible goal of forgetting. And then, mistakenly believing that they have not forgiven, feel guilty. That is not only sad, but tragically common among Christians. It provides an incubator in which Satan can hatch destructive doubts about the reality of our faith.

The test of whether or not we have forgiven someone is not in whether or not we remember the incident, or even in whether or not there is some pain connected with the memory. Those leftover effects are common. The proof of forgiving lies in attitude and action.

God always responds to our honest, sensible efforts. He never asks us to do anything that is beyond our control. He will do with our memories whatever leads us to wholeness. After we have forgiven an injustice, whether we remember it once, frequently, or never, it is of no consequence—the wound is healed.

In summary, we don't forget. But, miracle of miracles, it no longer matters that we remember! We are no longer controlled by the hurt; we are no longer controlled by the desire to get even. We spring free through God's power helping us to forgive. Praise His name!

Now, let's learn how forgiving helped several individuals find new freedom, and how you can begin to find healing of your past and present wounds.

5 | Freedom From a Cage of Fear:
Jimmy and the Bullies

JIMMY CRESTON'S FATHER described him as "a standard-issue sixth grader with heavy-duty upholstery." Jimmy was typical for his age in many ways: he built plastic models, had quick hands on video games, and was a Three Stooges fan.

He was uniquely himself, too. He enjoyed being in his cluttered room tinkering with his chemistry set or collections and had tremendous curiosity. He believed there was always something interesting just around the corner. But going outdoors usually meant a trip to the library for Jimmy, and he cautiously avoided the playgrounds on the way there.

His father, Sgt. Clay Creston, was in the U.S. Army as a career. Jimmy got his curiosity from him, but his father had an adventurer's metabolism that Jimmy lacked. It had led him to join the army, to earn his airborne rating, and, after distinguished service through the ranks, to become an instructor at the paratrooper training center at Fort Benning. He stayed in the army out of patriotism and was an instructor because he was a strong leader.

Sergeant Creston and his family were just settling

into this new assignment when Jimmy began sixth grade. Jimmy had moved a lot, but this move was particularly difficult for him. And being forty pounds overweight is no advantage to a sixth-grade boy. On the first day of school, when Jimmy had bragged about his dad's career as a paratrooper, one of the boys, Rick, had retorted, "He must have fell on his head too many times to end up with a kid like you." That had cracked up the old timers.

Jimmy's mother, Corrine, was the kind of mother who "protected her brood." She meant well, but she overdid it. She had not found it easy to adjust to her husband's extended tours of duty. So during his assignments away, she had coped with her loneliness by cooking, eating, and feeding. Jimmy came by his strengths and weaknesses naturally.

The morning of the second day of school, Jimmy complained of an upset stomach. His mother prescribed an extra biscuit with strawberry jam. Jimmy walked very slowly to school and winced when he saw Rick, Joe, and Duane huddled near the door. There was no way to avoid them. Rick greeted Jimmy with mock friendliness. "Good morning, Blubber Gut, waddle over and I'll tell you a good joke. You'll love it. It's about a fat guy."

"I think I heard it."

"Yeah. That's right, you heard it. You're it!"

Jimmy's eyes and stomach burned. He fought tension in his hands that wanted to make fists and a welling urge to use those fists. He walked quickly in to take his seat.

That morning the science lesson was on whales. Jimmy heard his name whispered by Duane and heard Joe and Rick snicker. During the afternoon a paper clip whizzed by his ear. He had always thought it was unfair for new kids to have to sit up front. It was a long day, but he dreaded being dismissed and the hassles he might face walking home. As it turned out, The Three Stupids (as Jimmy was thinking of them) rode off on their bikes and Jimmy walked home uneasy, but without incident.

It was good to be back in the sanctuary of his room. Half an hour later he was astonished to see Duane, Joe, and Rick climb over the back fence. They took his bike, which had been leaning against the back of the house, and wheeled it to the center of the backyard, where they dropped it on its side. Rick kicked at the spokes of the front wheel with the heel of his shoe. "There's a better way than that." Duane said, and bashed the spokes of the back wheel with a piece of firewood. Joe was scraping paint off the frame with his knife blade.

Jimmy was incoherent with fear and anger. He raised the window to shout at them, but he was trembling so much he could muster only enough voice for a squeaky croak. "My dad will get you for this. Just wait 'til he finds out."

At that moment Jimmy saw his dad march around the corner of the house in full combat gear: olive-drab field uniform, rugged boots, camouflage-patterned helmet, and field pack with grenades dangling. The soldier quickly slipped his carbine from his shoulder and into combat-ready position. When he spoke to the boys it was all that Jimmy's threat had not been, and the boys took it as command. "Stand up facing me! Put both of your hands on top of your head! Don't make another move!" The boys obeyed immediately. Sergeant Creston's eyes burned brightly with the authority of a copper-clad magnum shell seen from the end of a large bore rifle.

Jimmy noticed with satisfaction that the boys were white with fear. His father barked an order to them.

"Now walk directly over to the side of the garage. Line up right there side by side. You have made fun of my son. You have hurt his property. You are guilty. You are being punished."

Jimmy's mouth dropped in disbelief. He wanted to shout "No, dad, don't do it! It wasn't that bad! We'll work it out!" But words didn't come. He wanted to run for help. He felt his legs thrashing, but he couldn't move. Again he tried to shout. This time the words came. "Mom! Mom! Come here quick! Don't let dad do it!"

His bedroom door opened. "What is it Jimmy?" his mother asked. "Did you have another bad dream?" She gently shook his shoulder.

Jimmy, lying on his back on top of his bed, looked up at his mother. He was trembling. Slowly, thankfully, he understood.

He saw a tear on his mother's cheek as she gently rubbed his shoulder. "It's not easy, is it Jimmy, to move to a new town? It isn't easy for me, either, but I'll help you every way I can."

"Mom, I try so hard, I just don't know what to do." He told her about school and about the dream. They both knew that he wanted to do what was right and that doing what was right would mean offering friendship in response to rejection, giving love in response to ridicule and indifference, being compassionate in the face of taunts and abrasiveness, and seeking to understand those who had ridiculed him. It was a tall order for a sixth-grade boy. But the family believed in doing right—that's what Jimmy's mother and father had taught him—and Jimmy had an uncommonly mature understanding of the power of love.

Jimmy understood what he needed to do but he didn't like it. "Mom, it isn't fair. It seems like I'm always the one who gets picked on and then I'm the one who has to do what's right. I wish God would strike wicked people dead like He used to do."

"God was like that in Old Testament times, but Jesus brought us a better way."

"It doesn't make sense to me to be nice to those guys when they've been so mean to me!"

"I know, Jimmy. But my experience has been that being nice is a better way, and I'm sure you'll learn that for yourself as you go through life. As Christians we often have to do the hard thing first, before we get the benefit. There is often some pain first and joy later. That is the opposite of the world's system where you get a little bit of fun first and then the pain later."

Jimmy listened carefully, frowning, weighing the alternatives. He knew he wanted revenge. Along with the terror in his dream there had been the illusion that revenge would be sweet and successful. The illusion was attractive.

Jimmy's mind and his mood were battling to control his behavior. If he decided what to do on the basis of what he felt, he would find a way to attack the three guys. He would have to be clever because he was badly outnumbered; but he would find ways to hurt them. If he did what he believed was right, he would forgive them and return love for the abuse they had given him.

He knew he wanted to do what was morally right. But that required strong active faith, and at that moment Jimmy didn't have faith that he could do what he knew he ought to do. But he knew where to get help.

"Mom, would you pray about it with me?"

His mother dried her tears on the bedspread as she knelt beside him.

The family was together for supper that evening. Jimmy talked with his dad about what had happened, and they briefly prayed together. Jimmy had no idea what to expect the next day. He knew it would be an adventure and he knew that he would survive; but no matter how he turned the situation over and over in his mind, the happy ending was thickly encrusted by fear—like a pearl encrusted in its ugly shell, unable to be seen.

Jimmy approached school the next morning not

only with dread, but also with determination. He had agreed within himself that he wasn't even going to think of Duane, Joe, and Rick as "The Three Stupids" anymore.

When Jimmy arrived at school, the three boys were preoccupied with a magazine and gave Jimmy no recognition. During social studies class an assignment for group projects was given. Students, in teams of four, were to develop a presentation about a foreign country and present it to the rest of the class. Students could choose their own groups.

"Jimmy, do you have any thoughts about who you'd like to be with in a group?" the teacher asked. "I can make assignments, but if you would like to choose, you may."

Jimmy responded decisively. "If it's all right with them, I'd like to be with Rick, Joe, and Duane."

The teacher saw surprised looks on the faces of the three boys. They exchanged puzzled glances and shrugged their shoulders at one another before Rick said slowly, "Yeah, sure. That's okay."

The groups had one class period to work together on their projects. Jimmy suggested they do their presentation on Korea, where he had lived for three years. So the boys began planning what they would do. Jimmy had many ideas about the project and he offered to bring photos and curios. The boys quickly realized that with Jimmy's help they could easily do a super job on the project. It seemed to them that it was too good to be true.

Rick put their suspicion into words. "What's with you, Jimmy? After the way we hassled you yesterday, why did you want to throw in with us?"

"Partly," Jimmy began explaining, "because of one of the things you said. When you said, 'Do you have any guts in that big gut of yours, Big Boy?' that got me thinking how a guy can't show anybody how tough he is by running away. And on the other hand, things never got any better for me when I gave a hassle when I got a hassle. So what else was there to do?"

Rick, Joe, and Duane looked at Jimmy blankly, trying to comprehend all they had heard. Rick shook his head slowly and thoughtfully. "You're not such a bad guy," he said.

Jimmy's mother was surprised when he came home smiling. "It must be easy for you. How do you do it?"

"I had a couple of helpers," Jimmy replied.

"I wish I did."

"You were one of them."

"Me?"

"Yeah. You said, 'Do what's right, what needs to be done, and the Lord will help you.' So, that's what I did."

"And it worked?"

Jimmy heard the surprise in her voice. "Of course." He continued, somewhat sadly. "Yeah, mom, sure. Don't you know that?"

"I guess I do and I don't. My head tells me yes, but my stomach tells me no." She reached for a cookie, then paused. "This is what I'll say no to and I'll say yes to doing what you did."

She sighed, smiling. "Jimmy, what say we take these cookies across the street and meet the neighbor?"

Through this incident Jimmy and his mother learned again the practical benefits of doing what is right. Corrine developed a very valuable friendship with her neighbor Hope, a perceptive and compassionate woman. As for Jimmy with Rick, Joe, and Duane? They didn't become friends. In fact, after the social studies project was finished they didn't have much to do with each other. Instead, Jimmy became friends with two boys whose interests were similar to his. In time, they came to refer to themselves as "The Three Musketeers."

Jimmy's experience illustrates three elements that frequently are part of the forgiving process. First, Jimmy made a conscious decision to do what was right, whether he felt like it or not. He was guided by his mind and his understanding of God's principles, rather than by his feelings. Second, he asked God for help. It usually does require God's help to do what we believe is right, rather than what we feel like doing. That help is, as Jimmy found out, available. Third, he was willing to become the servant of those who had hurt him. The process of forgiving began when Jimmy decided that he would try to do what was right. The process probably was completed when Jimmy put into practice his willingness to love those who had hurt him.

6 | Freedom From Tension in Marriage:
Ken and Ruth Make Up

KEN AND RUTH HEDDON were having what was, for them, just a routine discussion. An observer might have called it a fight, but Ken wouldn't have. After all, Christian education directors and their wives don't fight.

The highlight of Monday's discussion came when Ken said, "What would people think?"

Ruth exploded. "What would *people* think? I'll tell you what people think right now! I'm people, too, which you don't seem to know; so I'll tell you what I think—I think you stink! You don't listen to me. You don't ask my advice. Look at you now, ready to butt in and tell me how I'm wrong and you're right, like you always do. I'm sick of that. I'm sick of being treated like a hired hand. I'm sick of being told to shut up and not worry about it. I'm sick of—sick of—I'm sick of you, Mr. Christian Education. If you want to talk, you can talk to an empty room!"

Ruth stomped into the bedroom and slammed the door behind her. Ken slumped back in his chair and mentally reviewed his grievance, checking each bit of evidence. Yes, he concluded, it was *her* fault. He distinctly remembered reminding her to record that check in the checkbook.

The "suffer in silence" stage was of average length —two and one-half hours. It ended when a neighbor came over to borrow an egg.

Tuesday's "discussion" had no moments of high drama. It was uniformly sticky, like peanut butter, and as enjoyable as, well, a peanut-butter shampoo.

Ken was grumbling, "You could have explained yourself."

"I was trying to until you butted in. It's just—"

"I didn't. I only—"

"What do you call *that*! You butted in again!"

Ken sighed. "Well, I'm not perfect like you expect me to be. You told me in the morning I should dress better, like Pastor Raymond. I can't afford to dress better."

"You could if you didn't waste your money on stuff like a new bowling ball."

"What about you and your fancy sewing machine that was going to save you all that money? And last week you bought a new dress."

"Try to take care of two kids all day and have time to sew."

"The kids should be taking care of themselves by now."

"It would help if they had their father around more to discipline them."

"If you had disciplined them when they were younger like I told you to—"

Wednesday's "discussion" was brief. "You're too quiet," Ken said.

"You're too loud."

"I can change that." And he proceeded to set a new personal record for the length of the silent treatment.

Thursday was different. The children were in bed early, and Ken and Ruth were having a snack at the dinette.

Ruth looked at Ken with the limp expression of one who has given up caring about what happens. "Ken, when I think back over our six years of marriage, I see a long dusty road. That's where we've been, and all we have seen is the dust. We don't even know what's been along the way. That can't possibly be where we have to go. Something better must be possible for us."

Ken slowly pushed dishes away from him and laid his head on his arms on the table. "You're right," he said in a muffled voice. There was another long silence as they both toyed with the truth that was nudging them. Ken raised up slowly and reached out to touch Ruth's wrist.

"You're right, Ruth. We've bickered time and time again over nothing. We've compared each other with others who seem to be perfect. That way, all we see in each other is what appears to be imperfections and shortcomings. We end up looking at the dust instead of the destination.

"I want to quit comparing you with others. Instead, I'm going to try to compare myself with the one who is perfect—Christ—and strive to become more like Him. Let's go for it!"

They did. It took time and discipline, of course. Ken found some methods to help them, and one of the most helpful was praying together, specifically on behalf of their marriage. They would each pray aloud and include these elements in their prayers:

> Praise of God
> Affirmation of partner
> Thanks to God for partner
> Repentance of sins against partner
> Request for God's help in fulfilling responsibilities
>   to partner

In time they discovered a pattern that had created conflict for them. They had entered marriage with unrealistic expectations about what marriage should be like. They made comparisons with other couples; but because they had such limited information about them, the comparisons were unrealistic. Nevertheless, they had a lot of envy and dissatisfaction, which led to more demands on one another, squabbles, retaliation, and resentment.

They discovered that when God entered the marriage at a practical level things changed. They could, and would, apologize and forgive. As the pain of past grievances faded away, there was more incentive to give loving care to the other. As they quit adding new wounds, trust grew, and with that came freedom to be vulnerable and spontaneous.

They got acquainted! They met each other. They met themselves. Infatuation matured to love.

A year later Ken and Ruth were sitting at the dinette. "Remember the time you called me 'Mr. Christian Education?'" Ken asked.

"Yes."

"I didn't like that."

"Of course not. I was being as sarcastic as I knew how to be."

"You may have meant to be sarcastic but you were accurate—that's what hurt. I was married to my work and was always trying to play the role of educator in our marriage. Now we're both students of Christ—in our marriage and in life."

"That works!"

"Yeah!"

"Want to fight so we can kiss and make up?"

"Let's skip the fight."

Ken and Ruth had finally developed the attitudes and skills of a good marriage. The first task for them had been to learn that good relationships come by taking personal responsibility for conforming to the image of Christ, rather than by demanding that the other person conform to the image of another person. They also needed to learn to apologize and to forgive.

It's tough to forgive! It is especially difficult to forgive those who are most important to us. There are several reasons why it is difficult for us to forgive:

1. By nature we are selfish and proud. And, as mentioned previously, forgiving requires unselfishness and humility.

2. Forgiving is often interpreted as weakness in today's American culture. We seldom understand Christ's example of strength through servanthood; instead we accept violence and revenge as normal, reasonable responses to injustice.

3. Not forgiving seems to have some benefits. An immature sense of satisfaction comes from "licking our wounds" in self-pity. Vengeance gives a cheap thrill. Not forgiving is easier, briefly, than forgiving. The wound may be used to make others feel sorry for us. These seeming benefits of not forgiving are deceptive, and they keep us from enjoying the true benefits of forgiving.

4. Fear is a huge barrier. When the person we need to forgive is very important to us, we may fear losing the good aspects of our relationship; or we may believe that forgiving the other person will increase the chances that he or she will hurt us again. We may be afraid of this unknown experience of forgiving, of doing the wrong thing, of looking foolish before others. We may be afraid that if we act mature this time, we will have to live up to it in the future. And we may even be so unfamiliar with contentment that we are afraid to give up the more familiar feeling of resentment.

5. Recognizing our own guilt and realizing that we must apologize for our offenses keeps us from forgiving. Again, it comes down to fear and pride.

6. The emotional hurt may be so intense that it is difficult to think logically and to take the actions

necessary for forgiving. Feelings should not control our lives, but at times they are so intense they interfere with our ability to plan seriously or to carry out our plans.

When Ken and Ruth did not apologize and forgive, the driving force of their marriage was competition, not cooperation. It was very costly to them.

Not forgiving is always costly. It interferes with our fellowship with God and with our fellowship with others. That is why Scripture so clearly commands that we apologize and forgive, and that we do so promptly.

7 | Freedom From Resentment:
Tom and His Ex-wife

TOM NORRIS WAS sitting in the center of the living-room floor of his cluttered one-bedroom apartment talking to his five-year-old daughter, Julie. "Daddy didn't want your mom to leave. When we got married I loved her; I tried hard for nine years to give her a good marriage and to get her to love me. When she left me, you were only three, too young to understand. Andy was just six then, and it was hard enough for him to understand. Believe me, Julie, I wish we were all still together. I would give anything for that.

"What your mother says isn't true, that's all there is to it. I love you and Andy and sometimes I still love your mother, too, even after what she did to me. I'm a good man, Julie; I love you. I'm never going to hurt you. I never did anything to hurt your mother. She just decided she wanted to leave, that's all.

"She said she wanted to do her own thing, to discover who she really was as a woman. She thought living with me was too boring, just because I'm a guy who believes he ought to go to work when he's supposed to be there. See," he said sarcastically, "I have some funny ideas like that. I believe in honesty, fair play, and hard work—things that your mother doesn't care about. Well, I guess that's her business—. But, Julie, it is my business to make sure you and I get along with each other. You're my daughter; Andy is my son; and I love you both.

"Andy! You and me, we're good buddies, right?" Tom spoke with hopeful enthusiasm.

Andy, sprawled on the sofa reading a Spiderman comic, mumbled, "Right, dad," and turned the page.

Tom turned back to Julie. "Your mother fills your minds with poison and sends you over to hurt me with those lies she has taught you. I don't blame you two for that, but I do want you to understand why I can't let this go on." He checked his watch. "We gotta get you back to your mother's place."

Tom drove slowly, engulfed by the sadness he always felt when visitation was over. He walked to the door with Julie and Andy. When Bette answered he said sarcastically, "Here are your mercenaries."

"It's bad enough you're their father. You don't have to insult my children," Bette replied.

"I'm not. I'm insulting you, if you were only bright enough to understand it."

"You always have had a way of attacking everyone."

"All I'm doing is pointing out the truth. That's fair enough. Not like you—you attack me with your actions."

"Like?"

"Bringing the kids late this morning."

"You're late now."

"Wrong. I was to have them eight hours. I did. And no more."

"They were to be back at four o'clock, and it's almost five."

"Yeah. Exactly eight hours after you brought them."

"You're an uptight nitpicker. If you cared about the kids, you'd treat their mother better."

"And if *you* cared about them, you'd give me custody. Then they would at least have one parent." He walked to his car.

"Come see me again, lover boy," Bette called to him with mock sweetness.

Tom fumed as he drove recklessly back to his apartment. He sat on the floor, his back against the couch, and called Liz Adams, a woman he had been dating for several months. After small talk, the conversation got serious.

"She brought them late, so I returned them late. Oh, listen to that! *Returned* them. *Return* is something you do with library books. That's what makes me so flippin' mad. Bette's turned those kids into puppets in a war. Bad enough what she did to me, running off with that putty-faced psychopathic liar—and marrying that meathead."

Liz replied with venom. "If you ever did to me what she keeps doing to you, I would ruin you for life. I'd hurt you in every way you could be hurt—I'd take you for every penny, I'd drag your name in the mud, I'd hurt you physically if I could, and I'd kidnap my kids. Until you hurt her, she's going to continue hurting your kids and hurting you."

Tom saw the point. If the principle of an eye for an eye ever seemed justified, he thought, surely it was in his case.

Liz continued. "You couldn't trust her from the day you met her, Tom. Every time you gave her an inch, she took you for a mile. You can't let that go on."

Tom knew that he couldn't let it continue, but he didn't know what to do about it.

There was only one other person in whom Tom had ever confided. That was Ray Lewis, who worked in the same shop where Tom worked. Tom knew that Ray found a lot of strength in his Christian faith. Tom didn't understand that, but he admired Ray.

The first time Tom found Ray alone at a coffee break, he wasted no time getting to the point. "Ray, what would you do if you had somebody hassling you time after time? Would you just grin and bear it?"

"Absolutely not. If somebody does something to hurt me, that's wrong; so I ought to try and prevent them from continuing to do something wrong. I have that responsibility to them and I also have a responsibility to myself not to let myself be abused." He paused, noticing that Tom nodded his understanding. "Somebody hassling you?"

"The ex."

"That can really be painful."

"Uh-huh, and especially when it involves my kids. Especially when it doesn't stop. And especially when she does it on purpose." He saw concern in Ray's eyes, so he continued. "What can I do about it?"

"The thing most people would want to do first—at least the urge that comes to me first—is to get even, to hurt them right back."

"Sure! I think about that a lot!"

"Have you done it?"

"No. I really haven't." He thought a moment. "I get pretty ugly with my words. But I pay my child support on time and I haven't hit her."

"Good! Hurting them back is wrong, of course. And it doesn't work, either. Often, the hardest part is not doing the things you feel like doing—not letting your feelings dominate your mind. Because if your mind doesn't stay in control, you may lose control of your behavior; and then the mess is a whole lot bigger."

"Well, so far so good on that score. But—"

"But you're wondering how much longer you can hang on?"

"Exactly."

"Well, if you will allow me a commerical break, that's where being a Christian helps me tremendously.

It has made it possible for me to get through some rough places in life. I don't know how I would have gotten through some of them if it hadn't been for the help I get through my Christian faith. I recommend it. End of plug."

"If you're onto something good, don't hide it."

"What I'd like to do is tell you more about it. Could we get together for a meal one day soon?"

They did. There was a lot of conversation between them during the next several months, and on several occasions, Liz and Carol Lewis were included as well.

In the beginning Ray was primarily trying to help Tom avoid making big mistakes and to support him through this awkward period. As Tom's interest and understanding grew, Ray began teaching him about salvation in a balanced way. But Tom had a lot of objections. Having his sins forgiven didn't seem very important to Tom because he didn't feel he had sinned. And forgiving Bette for her sins, especially seventy times seven, didn't appeal to him at all. "I think I was meant to have lived in Old Testament times," Tom said. "That appeals to me a lot more."

"It appeals to our sinful nature, all right," Ray explained, "but after we believe in Christ, we understand why the new way is a better way. As I've been telling you, there are some things you have to take on faith at this point. You make a decision in faith and discover later, just as I have, that things work out exactly as the Bible says they will."

Tom checked out everything. "You mean Liz couldn't live with me on weekends?"

"That's correct."

"You mean I have to treat Bette with respect?"

"You try to treat her the way Christ treats you."

"Oh, wow, I couldn't do that!"

"Not by yourself, that's for sure. Fortunately you have Christ's help available to you."

Tom decided to believe in, and live for, Christ. Then he discovered, a little at a time, that Ray was right—Christ did help him become more patient and cooperative with Bette. He amazed himself one day by apologizing to her for his lack of cooperation and his part in their petty bickering. He felt very good about that, but every time he thought of how she had rejected him and the humiliation it had caused him, anger surged within him. He had hateful thoughts toward her and he knew that he had not forgiven her. Good works had not been enough.

He talked to Ray about it. "I'm doing everything right, Ray, but the old problems keep bugging me. I'm keeping my behavior under control, but, in spite of that, I haven't won the battle. What's missing?"

Ray explained that forgiving is an act of the will. Tom had made a deliberate, conscious decision to change his behavior, but he had not made the same deliberate, conscious decision to forgive her for what she had done. For Tom, to stop doing wrong was a commendable and necessary step; but he had not yet, by an act of his will, forgiven her. Ray's advice to him was to forgive, claim it, close it, and keep it closed.

Tom decided that was what he wanted to do, but he didn't think he could. So he prayed, "Lord, I don't really want to forgive Bette, but I know that I should. I do want to be obedient to you. Because I want to be obedient to you, I ask you to help me want to forgive her. I'm willing to want to, even though it seems impossible now. Please take my willingness to want to forgive and change it into a real wanting to forgive, so that I can do it."

Tom stepped as far as he could. It wasn't a very big step, but it was all that he could do; and that's all the Lord ever expects of us. When Tom used his will, to the extent that he could, to do what was right, the Lord helped him with the rest of it. Tom knew that he had forgiven her. He claimed it, considered it closed, and determined to keep it closed. As a result, Tom enjoyed peace he had never before experienced.

Two weeks later, however, Ray heard a knock at his door—an urgent knock—and opened it to find Tom, livid and distressed.

"Bette's done it to me again! This is the most rotten stunt of all time!" He spoke frantically, with wild, brittle gestures. He was breathing rapidly, almost to the point of hyperventilation, and there was a wild look in his eye that Ray had never seen before.

"Ray, I can't take this. She's gone crazy and she's trying to drive me crazy! This is the most insane thing that woman has ever done," and he waved a letter in the air.

The letter was from an attorney stating Bette was pregnant, alleging Tom as the father, and threatening to sue him for child support. The letter went on to say that Bette, being a responsible person, preferred to spare Tom the inconvenience of legal action and that it would be to his advantage to voluntarily come to the attorney's office and agree to conditions.

"Ray, I swear to you I have not touched that woman since the day she walked out on me. I thought she had hurt me every way she could, but she's found a new way."

They talked for quite a while and then Tom said, "I think the thing that hurts the most is that I thought I had forgiven her and now I find I haven't. Look at me, as angry as I ever was."

"Tom, the fact that you are angry over this does not change the forgiving that you have already done. You are angry about a new wound. It's understandable you're angry about that. Don't for a minute think the feelings you have now change the forgiving you have already done. They don't. Again, you will be guided by your will in this. And I believe you will again decide to forgive. There has to be a way out of this mess. Together we'll find it."

They did, although things were in turmoil for a long time. When Bette's child was born, Tom volunteered for a blood test. At that point Bette dropped her false accusation.

Tom grew spiritually during this time, was able to control his own behavior, and worked hard at developing relationships with Julie and Andy. Those relationships blossomed.

Meanwhile, Bette got enmeshed in a circle of friends who were heavily involved in drug abuse, sex, and marginal living. She was apprehended for child neglect, and the infant was placed in a foster home. Tom was given custody of Julie and Andy. When that happened he said to Ray, "I've prayed to have my children with me, but not at this cost. It breaks my heart to see what Bette has done to herself." He prayed for her regularly.

Forgiving changes us; it does not change the other person. Forgiving heals past wounds; it does not protect us from future wounds.

Forgiving the second time may be harder, and the third time even more difficult. So do we quit forgiving? No, we follow the principle Christ taught Peter, that we always forgive (Matt. 18:21–35). This does not mean, as you will read in chapter 14, that we condone wrong behavior or leave ourselves unprotected against future hurt.

But we must recognize that forgiving may take place over a long period of time. It may be a cycle repeated over and over in a relationship with a friend or family member. Unfortunately, there is no special process that makes this repetitive forgiving any easier— there is no quantity discount. Here's what we can do:

1. Begin where we can begin. Forgive what we can forgive.

2. Pray for willingness to forgive the rest.

3. As we can, forgive the rest.

4. Don't be surprised if we remember more old offenses or if new offenses occur. Deal with them one by one. Recycle points two and three above.

Even when there have been many offenses, there may be only one occasion when the forgiver talks with the other person about forgiving, and maybe not even one. But even if there are more opportunities, they should often be avoided because they are not necessarily constructive to the other person. The Lord will guide us in knowing when to discuss with the other person our forgiving of his or her sins against us. The essential element of forgiveness is our heart attitude, not the words spoken to the other person, important as those words may be.

When we are wounded the second time, our feelings are probably going to be similar to the feelings we had the first time, and are likely to be even more intense. But these feelings do not mean we never forgave the first time. The feelings are not wrong and they do not necessarily indicate we have done wrong. We control our behavior and ultimately resolve unpleasant feelings by a process—forgiving—that begins with an act of the will.

8 | Freedom From an Empty Childhood:
Zeno the Ambitious

DIAMOND'S WAS THE most elegant department store in the city, the cosmetic and jewelry department the most elegant in the store, and the manager of that department, Zeno Daye, the most elegant objet d'art among the glittering, gorgeous baubles in her department. She was neither for sale nor a bauble. Fiercely independent, she used her beauty, intelligence, and street savvy to produce a glittering, gorgeous profit for the store.

The statuesque, auburn-haired young woman looked around the department with satisfaction. She smiled to herself as she thought about what she had accomplished in six years. She thought about the rich suburb and the fashionable home in which she had been raised. She was Darlene Dawson then, wallowing in possessions, receiving everything but affection from her parents. That was when she had created her new name and couldn't wait until she was old enough to have it legally changed. And it was then she had developed the fantasy of independence and power she was shaping into reality now.

She began modeling for Diamond's during high

school. After a year at business college, she decided she could learn faster on the job. She did. She used her beauty to intimidate and to attract. Many men had ideas about how they could help advance her career, but she had waited patiently to snare the man who could benefit her the most: Jordon Holt III, vice president for merchandising.

Zeno decided to base her security on money and power. On the job she was capable, enthusiastic, and successful; and she was promoted rapidly. Although she admitted money wasn't everything, she said that having it sure made it easier to enjoy the rest.

Her thoughts were broken as Jordon Holt walked by. "Hello, Ms. Daye," he said with the same bland smile and greeting he gave the housekeepers, the newest cashier, the guys in receiving. She had to laugh at his deception—she hoped it was deception. Then she thought, what business is it of theirs if Jordy and I spend every Thursday evening together? It's good for him; it sure has helped my career; and, as for his wife, if she doesn't like it, it's her own fault.

Among department heads she was as competent as any and was advancing the most rapidly. She was also the most admired, the most envied, and the least happy. She tried to keep her unhappiness submerged beneath activities. She attended plays and art shows—to be seen, not to see—and listened greedily to motivational tapes. But an aching sense of aimlessness kept trying to surface, and she dimly knew that its causes included more than the death of her parents in a private plane crash a year ago. She put those thoughts aside and decided to go out for a quiet supper and to come back after the store had closed to study her financial reports.

She walked two blocks to Leonardo's, a small, expensive restaurant. She wanted to be alone to sort out her feelings. Despite her pride and satisfaction in what she had accomplished, she had the uneasy sense that the foundation of her achievement was about to crumble.

Entering the dim, quiet restaurant she saw Ben Marks, manager of the Housewares Department, beckon to her. Although she had never had any major conflict with Ben, she was not particularly comfortable with him. Reluctantly she joined him. As they ate she made small talk of minor complaints about management and company gossip and noticed, irritably, his optimism and the way he steered the conversation back to neutral topics. Her disappointment over not being able to eat alone grated on her, and she resented his positive attitude.

Deciding to unsettle and intimidate him, she said bluntly "You're gay, aren't you?"

"No," he said casually, "but that *used* to be my lifestyle."

"I knew it. From the first time I met you, I knew it." She spit the words on him and leaned toward him defiantly, hoping to see hatred in his eyes. She saw only the reflection of her own.

He replied humbly, "You must really want to hurt me. If that's what you want, do us both a favor. Let's talk about what's going on—*really* going on."

"Why should I talk to you about anything that's my personal business?" she snapped back. It was meant as a slap, but they both heard the cry for help within it. "Why should I trust you?"

His eyes were gentle and honest as he looked tenderly into her eyes. "Because I care that you hurt so bad inside. Because I understand your pain. Because I've been there. Because I know there is a better way."

She wanted to believe him. "What's your pitch?" she asked gruffly.

"You feel hollow. You feel like you're worthless. You're not, of course, but you feel that way; so you fill up your life with power and money. It isn't working. Power and money are like cotton candy. You need a balanced diet. I'll bet you never got the emotional nourishment you needed as a kid. I'll bet your folks gave you everything except themselves. Right?"

"Well—I guess you're right, but—"

"No. Wait a sec, please, you need to hear what happened to me."

"Spare me the sordid details."

"Will you listen to the good news?"

"Is there a choice?"

"Sure."

She saw a strength in him she had never seen before—confidence and honesty. "Go ahead, but quickly."

"My life was a mess—bad enough that I figured suicide was too good for me. I knew why it was a mess. Just like you, I was trying to fill an empty place with the wrong attitudes and the wrong behavior. My pattern was different than yours on the surface, but in substance it was the same problem."

"I'm pretty sure I don't agree with you, but I think I understand your point of view."

"Willing to hear more?"

"If it's quick."

"I made a religious commitment—"

"Oh, wow, here it comes."

"Yes, Zeno, here comes the good news: the decision I made about a year ago to accept Jesus Christ as Savior and Lord of my life totally changed my life."

"And now your sins are whiter than snow."

"You know what I'm talking about, don't you?"

"I've been to Sunday school."

"Then I assume you know that God's forgiveness is complete and that His provision for our eternal life in heaven is sure. But you also need to realize there is still the matter of everyday living that needs to be taken care of—especially for people like you and me. Here's what I mean. I had a tremendous empty place that love from my family should have filled when I was growing up. Like you, right?"

"Yeah."

"Even after I accepted Christ I still had that empty place and I still had problems with hatred and with controlling my behavior. That's all different now. Even the pain I had from a long time ago has been taken care of."

"How could that be?"

"God isn't limited in time or space, so He can go back in time and take care of things like that. He did it for me. He filled up the emptiness that was in my life fifteen, eighteen years ago—through prayer."

"You're getting a little bizarre, and that turns me off."

"Okay, look. You believe there is God?"

"Yes."

"That He is the creator of the universe?"

"Yes."

"That He does take personal interest in people?"

"Yes."

"That's all pretty bizarre itself, isn't it? Pretty hard to imagine? Pretty hard to understand?"

"Yeah."

"You still believe it?"

"I guess so." She pondered a moment. "Yeah, I really do."

"So why not believe just a tiny bit more if it can make a gigantic difference in your life? Why not use all you believe if it can change your life from miserable to fantastic?"

"I'll tell you why. Because I don't want God to take away everything I've worked hard for the last six years. Because I don't want to end up a fat, tired, grumpy complainer."

"Which is what all Christians are?"

"A lot of them, you have to admit."

"Sure, I'll admit that, and they're a royal turn-off, but there are a bunch who aren't. I want you to meet—"

"Look, thanks for your life's story. It's cute. I believe you and I believe you believe it all, but I need to get back to the store. It's been nice, but I've got things I have to do."

She grabbed her check and hurried to the cashier. Ben started to follow, but settled back to think and pray.

Zeno avoided Ben the rest of the week. She even took a long detour through Men's Wear to avoid walking through Housewares enroute to the Personnel Department, an unprecedented waste of two minutes. The pressure she felt was unprecedented, too, especially the nagging sense that Ben was right.

Thursday evening with Jordon Holt was a disaster. They argued; and each threatened to publicly humiliate the other, something they both knew they could never do. Her powerlessness in this situation dawned on her for the first time. She reacted first with frustration, then with anger, and finally with fear—a clammy realization that her strategies were not working.

She tried to direct her anger toward Ben, but the sense that he was right continued to deflect the anger back toward her. And that aggravated her more.

Several weeks after their first supper at Leonardo's, Zeno saw Ben there again. She was just beginning her salad when he came in. He looked hopefully in her direction, their eyes met for a moment, then she looked back at her salad without giving him as much as a nod of recognition.

The headwaiter began leading Ben to a small table, but before they reached it Zeno yelled, breaking the mannerly atmosphere for which Leonardo's was noted, "Ben! Over here!"

All eyes in the room turned toward her and then toward Ben, who was standing frozen in his tracks. He gave a cautious smile like a small boy wondering whether or not he was being apprehended for an unknown crime.

"Would the gentleman care to be seated with the—ah—lady?" the headwaiter asked. Ben nodded, and was led to the seat across from Zeno.

She blushed and looked furtively around the room. This was the first time Ben had seen her in less than complete command of her performance.

Ben spoke. "Thanks. It's nice to join you."

"I didn't know if you would want to talk to me again."

He smiled. "Imagine that! And me thinking the same thing about you."

"I'll tell you straight out. I thought about what you said. If it's true, you've had a lot of success, and I never argue with success—I never argue with the facts. On the other hand, some of the hocus-pocus part of it is hard for me to swallow."

"I think I didn't explain myself very well. What I wanted to show you was that you already believe a lot about the supernatural. You believe that God created the world, that He exists now, and that He takes a personal interest in us. To me it doesn't seem like a much bigger step to believe that He can and will change our lives for the better, if we let Him—and a little bigger step to let Him do that. It's hard to trust Him, and maybe for you it's even harder to stop trusting in your own capabilities."

"That was true enough two or three weeks ago. Maybe it's not as true now. Some things have happened."

"If I took a quick guess, I'd say you are finding that the foundation of your system is crumbling."

"Maybe something like that." The waiter brought

Zeno's entrée and took Ben's order. They made small talk about Zeno's food, broiled mahi-mahi, and talked shop before the conversation moved back to personal matters.

"Ben, you know how in our industry there are salespeople and there are service reps? You know no matter what they say, salespeople are always trying to hustle the product. They have commissions and quotas; so, naturally, they want to score on you. That's the name of their tune. Service reps operate under different rules, so they can treat you differently. They can help you in whatever way is best for you." She leaned forward with a wry smile. "Ben, why does the God business have all salespeople and no service reps?"

Ben laughed out loud. His laughter was partly of joy, for he heard honest inquiry within her question, and partly of embarrassment, for he recognized mistakes of his own in her observation.

"Love it! Love the question! I suppose there are a lot of people pushing the product for the wrong reasons. I know there are a lot of people who push it and push it hard because of what it has done for them. Maybe I'm in that category, too. I'll tell you for sure, though, that as honest as I can be with myself I really do want you to have what is really good for you. But there are service reps, too. I meet with a whole group of them—people who have become my friends, who teach me, who encourage me, and who unselfishly counsel and support me for no reason other than they want what is best for me. These are credible people, Zeno, not kooks. The kind of people you could respect. I wish—"

"Is this the conversation we had before?"

"No, because in this conversation you're going to say, 'I'll think about it.'"

"Aren't you the crafty one? Okay, I'll think about *what*?"

"About having dinner here one night next week with Keith and Jean, a couple of friends from my group. What do you say?"

"I'll think about thinking about it."

"Aren't you the crafty one! But I love it! Love the answer!"

They did have dinner the following week. And again the next week. And the next. And the next.

Along the way, Zeno's mistrust of Ben, Jean, and Keith began to melt away. Images of a new kind of lifestyle began to form in her mind. She began to understand principles of the Christian faith, and she began believing that God could indeed be trusted.

She saw with painful clarity the emptiness of her childhood. She recognized her longings for affection that had never been fulfilled by her parents and understood that she had tried to fill that longing with money and power; she saw how she had used physical intimacy—the illusion of affection—to gain that power.

One week, in silent defiance, Zeno did not meet Jordon Holt III for their Thursday evening rendezvous. He walked through her department the next morning, gave his usual bland greeting, and nothing more was ever said.

That was the beginning of tangible change, because healing begins when we forsake wrong behavior. When Holt was out of the picture, Zeno realized what an emotional drain that alliance had been. Now she was free emotionally, and in time she talked and studied more with her new Christian friends. About a year after her first conversation with Ben, Zeno invited Christ into her life as Lord and Savior. It happened, by the way, in a booth at Leonardo's. After an honest prayer, Zeno brushed away mascara-stained tears and, smiling at her friends, said triumphantly, "A new Daye begins!"

Her friends knew that the emotional emptiness she

had endured as a child remained. They prayed about this regularly as part of their Bible-study meetings. They gathered around the person being prayed for and each person prayed silently as the group members took turns praying aloud. Zeno would always begin by asking God to make her aware of things she needed to learn about her life in order to live more completely in harmony with His principles. They all prayed this regularly. On some occasions Zeno had clear memories of lonely childhood experiences and of feeling rejected. Then the group would pray specifically that the needs of that age period would be filled.

Zeno found herself feeling stronger and more complete after each occasion. One evening she had a definite sense that the deficiencies from her childhood development had been compensated for and that the foundation of her life was finally complete.

But she still had to contend with the present. There were new temptations and plenty of pressures from the old ones. Ben explained the principle of displacement to her. "The way to push out the undesirable is to bring in something better. You've been doing that already, so you know it works."

"What do you mean?"

"Think of it this way: which did more to improve your life—Thursdays with Holt or Thursdays with Jean, Keith, Ben, and the Bible?"

"No contest!"

"But if it hadn't been for what we learned together, wouldn't it have been difficult to give up Holt?"

"Sure! I see what you mean—crowd out sin by bringing in Christ!"

"You've got it! Aren't you the crafty one!"

The present is affected, for better or for worse, by what has happened to us in the past. It may also be affected by what has not happened, especially when an important need, such as a child's need for parental nurturing and reassurance, is not met. That was Zeno's situation.

She tried to fulfill that need through money, power, and sex. None worked. But when she put Christ at the center of her life, it was possible to bring contentment into emptiness. As she put it, "haughtiness is hollowness; humility brings happiness."

After her conversion Zeno brought her behavior under control. She also became aware of her anger toward her parents for emotionally isolating her during childhood and for abandoning her by their accidental deaths. When she forgave them for those unintentional wounds, the wounds remained. They were healed by the Lord in response to prayer by Zeno and her friends.

Forgiving is necessary for wounds to be healed. What about talking with the person we are forgiving?

Sometimes we can't talk. The other person may be dead, as in the situation with Zeno. The person may refuse the invitation to talk. The person may be physically distant (although you can now direct dial every major country in the world). Or, while we may be able to meet face-to-face, the other person might be unable to participate emotionally or mentally either because of lack of motivation or the lost capacity to be involved.

Sometimes we should talk. We have a *right* to tell others they have hurt us. And we have a *responsibility* to tell Christians so they do not continue to sin against us. See Luke 17:3 for a clear statement about this.

Sometimes we shouldn't talk. In Luke 17:3–4 we see that we do not talk with the other person about the forgiving unless that person repents. And even then it is likely to make the other person uncomfortable in some way—perhaps embarrassed, indignant and angry, or shamed. It may bruise the person's ego. Common sense and Christian love dictate that we not talk if it would hurt the other person more than it would benefit.

Be very cautious when the hurt is immense, when the other person's ego is weak or the other person lacks emotional flexibility, when there is no way to compensate for the damage. This latter situation is common when parents have unintentionally hurt children.

The only way to know whether or not we should talk with the person is to ask for and receive direction from the Holy Spirit. But we are always to forgive. As a general rule we should: (1) always take the initiative to apologize for our sins; (2) rebuke the other person when appropriate; but (3) wait for the other person to repent before talking with them about forgiving.

God always provides the instructions we need to live right. He provides whatever healing is best for us. Praise His name!

9 | Freedom From Self-condemnation:
A Perfectionist Learns To Forgive Herself

MIKE'S PARTY GUESTS weren't sure why he was telling them all this, but there was no stopping him now. "She's such a bleepin' workaholic," he fumed, "she makes the rest of us—who put in an honest forty, forty-five hours a week—look like we're lazy. And the topper is this: she doesn't enjoy it, but she couldn't stop it if she tried. It's pretty sick as far as I'm concerned!"

His friends looked at him blankly and nodded in agreement. "If it were just her life it wouldn't matter," he went on, "but she gives being normal a bad name."

He paused, thinking. His listeners waited impatiently, hoping this conversation had run down, but Mike went on. He spoke with carefully weighed words and with a tone of voice that revealed that Sharon had become an intriguing mystery to him.

"See, I keep having this funny feeling that behind all that careful lab work, behind that serious concentration, there's a real lively lady ready to jump out and start living. She won't show it. She hides from life behind her work; she almost tries to blend into the woodwork.

"For example, the way she does her hair. It's some drab color I can't even remember, and she does it in some austere style that doesn't work for her at all. With a little attention to a few things like that, she could be very, very attractive. All she shows us in the lab is the personality of a test tube. I can't believe that's the way she wants it, but she doesn't give herself a chance."

The others would gladly have dropped the subject, but Dean said brashly, "You're turned on to this lady and don't know it, Mike. You pretend she's some kind of personality puzzle, an equation to be figured out, but I think there's more to it than that."

"No, you're reading too much into it. This was just idle talk. As for figuring people out like equations, Dean, what is it you were just doing to me?" The group laughed.

"Come on over by the piano," Mike invited, "and let's all sing."

In her apartment, Sharon moved away from her piano, exhausted. She didn't play for leisure or pleasure; she played only because she felt she had a responsibility, an obligation to keep her hard-won proficiency alive. She settled into the couch with the works of Cicero, wondering what her co-workers did on Friday evenings. She brushed the thought aside as frivolous and began studying.

To an invisible observer, Sharon's books and her cat would have appeared to be her best friends. And that probably would have been right. She kept up extensive correspondence with old college friends, but her letters described only her work.

Dean had been thinking for several days about Mike's description of Sharon. He had found excuses twice to detour from the Computer Center, where he worked, to the lab. He saw what Mike meant when he described Sharon as a butterfly afraid to come out of her cocoon. Mike's attitude about it troubled Dean.

When he got a chance to have lunch with Mike, he said, "I saw your mystery lady. She looks like a hard-working professional to me."

"And a good-looking one, too, isn't she?" Mike asked eagerly.

"Yeah."

"Now, if I can just figure out why she is so stand-offish, I can figure out what to do about it."

"You really are taking this on as a project, aren't you? You research and development guys are all alike. Give you anything with an element of the unknown and you want to figure it out and change it. But I think you are messing around where you shouldn't, Mike. I don't think you ought to butt in where you're not wanted."

"What difference does it make that I'm not wanted, if I'm needed?"

"Think of her, think of—"

"I *am* thinking of her."

"Hear me out. Think of her rights. Maybe she likes living the way she does."

"But it's not normal."

"She's a valuable professional. She's a good team member, you said so yourself. What gives you the right to decide whether or not she ought to talk and laugh more on the job? For all you know, she has a more exciting social life than you do."

"No way. She's living in Dull City."

"How do you know?"

"I can sense it. I'll tell you what. You give me a month to work on this, and I'll show you something pretty amazing."

"Professor Higgins, you better butt out before you mess up somebody's life."

"You'll see."

They both felt tense as they returned to their jobs. In the lab Mike watched Sharon carefully calibrating her instruments. She took a glass vial of viral culture from the centrifuge, held it to the light, and looked at it. Mike wondered what she was thinking.

She looked at the thick, yellowish-green layer of active material that had separated from the medium. She wondered what would happen if she drank it. She knew the effect, in all probability, would be irreversible. But she didn't know if death would be quick and painless or long and agonizing. If she were only sure, she thought, the decision would be easy.

Mike stepped beside her, unnoticed. "You must really love your work, Sharon, to do it all so well."

She jumped, almost dropping the vial. With a shaky hand she set it in a holder on the lab bench. "Oh, uh, yes, it's what I trained for, so naturally I give it my best. It's a challenge."

"Excuse me for startling you. I should have known you were concentrating." He smiled awkwardly, not knowing whether to retreat or to move on with his plan.

"Okay." She glanced around the lab. "I've been pretty busy lately. Not that I mind, but it has been sort of a treadmill. I really am pretty busy."

"Too busy to walk down the hall for a cup of coffee?"

"I ought to keep working. I should process this sample right now."

"How about stopping at the Bel-Aire with the rest of the gang after work tonight? We do that every other Friday, you know."

"Thanks, but I should probably get straight home. I have a lot of work piled up there. Besides, I might be late getting away from here."

"Mondays were made for doing Friday's work. I wish you'd stop with us. Let me ask you again this afternoon."

"Okay, but I'd better get busy now."

Mike was as persistent with his "Case of Sharon"

as she was with her lab procedures. He was back a little before quitting time.

"We all want you to come. It's the Bel-Aire, right after work. Know where it is?"

"Yes, but—"

"But we don't want to disappoint our friends, do we?"

"I have a lot to close up. You'd probably be gone before I could finish and get there. Maybe another time."

"Hey, we'll be there. When you get in the door, just listen for the laughing, that's us."

"Maybe another time. I have a lot I should finish here."

"I hope you'll come," Mike said, feeling defeated. "See you later, I hope."

Sharon debated with herself for half an hour after quitting time. She was angry with envy at the personal freedom the others seemed to have, and with her envy came a sudden surge of rebellion she had never felt before.

"Why not?" she said emphatically, startled at her spontaneity. She slipped off her white lab coat, let it fall to the floor, walked out of the lab without turning out the light, and drove directly to the Bel-Aire. As she approached the front door, Mike, Dean, and Ellie walked out.

"Wow! You came! I'm glad you did! It's a little quiet here, so we're moving the party to The Wild Onion just down the street. The rest of the gang is already down there, probably half bombed by now. Let's catch up. Leave your car here, Sharon. Ellie, won't you change your mind and come along?"

Ellie saw that Sharon's discomfort matched her own. "Let's give Sharon a choice," she said to Mike. And turning to Sharon she said, "If you want, you and I could stay here."

Mike glared at Ellie and jangled his car keys near Sharon's eyes. "Direct flight to The Wild Onion and from there to Fantasy Island, boarding now."

Without hesitation and with perfect synchronism, Sharon and Ellie turned away from Mike and entered the Bel-Aire.

Seated facing each other in a booth, they were both a bit surprised at being there. "Sharon, two minutes ago I felt like I didn't know you at all; suddenly I feel like we understand each other very well."

"Maybe we do. But if you'd rather—"

"I'd rather be right here than doing anything else right now. What I would really like would be for you to tell me a little about yourself. I'd really like to get to know you better."

That is how a very strong friendship began. Over a period of many months, Ellie and Sharon developed a great deal of trust in one another. Sharon had, for the first time in her life, someone to whom she could tell her deepest fears, frustrations and dreams. Ellie, a warm-hearted Christian, was able to help Sharon find reconciliation with God, with herself, and with her family.

Sharon's father had also been a research scientist. His job was his life. He believed you should put all you have into it and leave some knowledge behind. Sharon's sister, nine years older than she, fit his philosophy exactly. She earned a Ph.D. in biochemistry in record time and was considered a rising superstar in her field.

When Sharon was ten, her father had begun receiving large royalties from a process he had developed, so Sharon was transferred to the most academically elite private schools. Her parents apparently reasoned that if older sister did well with ordinary opportunity, Sharon should do even better with superior opportunity. Sharon had tutors, private foreign language lessons, and piano lessons twice a week. She received everything except permission to have fun and the understanding that she was valuable whether her performance was superior or not. As a result, Sharon was miserable in a career chosen for her by her father; her self-esteem rose and fell in proportion to the amount of work she got done; she lacked the ability to get personal renewal from friendship and fun; she lived in fear of failure; she suffered from long-standing resentment toward her sister, even though she was not aware of it; and she was beginning to believe that things could never be better.

Ellie began teaching Sharon about God's forgiveness. The concept of God's grace, of salvation as a gift, appealed to Sharon; but she found it difficult to believe it was available to her. After much instruction, Ellie encouraged Sharon to make a faith decision about Christ. But Sharon was still saying things like "Maybe I should wait until I've gone to church for a year" and "What do you think about me doing volunteer work with impoverished people for a year to broaden my perspective on life, first?"

Then one day it happened. Sharon made a clearcut decision to receive God's forgiveness. At that moment, Sharon's searching ended and her growth began. Although there haven't been many occasions of high drama or sudden change, since that occasion there has been steady development.

Within a year she had joined a tennis club, her hair was a color you'd never forget, and she was dating a widower with two children. One of her childhood dreams, about which she had felt guilty until recently, was going to come true. She was going to have a family and be a piano teacher working in her own home. In the meantime, with self-criticism gone, she was accomplishing more in the lab in forty hours than she had before in fifty-five hours.

"Amazing, isn't it," she bubbled, "how the Lord can help us in everyday life? And how it changes all our other relationships? Like Mike and me. He and Dean have some private joke about me that I'll probably never understand. Something to the effect that Mike has made me what I am. Well, I'm having a chance to talk to him about serious things now, so we'll see what happens. Praise the Lord!"

Then she laughed, embarrassed. "That surprised me. I never said that before! It just popped out. Well, we change, don't we! Praise the Lord!"

"Perfectionists" are those who think they must perform without flaw, will scold and punish themselves if this unattainable goal is not met, and consequently will feel a sense of failure, worthlessness, pressure, anger, and depression. Sharon had a textbook case of this disorder.

She was so caught up in striving to be exceptional that she found it difficult to enjoy others, to pursue what she really wanted to do, and to become herself. She was on her way toward whole living when she forgave her parents for their loving blunders. They had pushed her into things in which she had no interest and had not helped her discover the freedom that comes from a proper amount of leisure time. Then she accepted God's grace and was able to forgive herself for scolding herself for failing to accomplish the impossible. And she was finally able to allow her own life to unfold, in God's direction, into the ideal pattern for her.

The perfectionistic pattern usually begins with the example of an influential person, usually a parent, who has the power to give rewards for outstanding performance and to give rejection when performance is less than satisfactory. These mentors usually have good intentions: they have a strong desire for the other person to be successful.

One of the worst things about being a perfectionist is that it does not work. Studies show that those with perfectionistic tendencies do not perform as well as those who are able to accept their own mistakes. Trying to be perfect almost guarantees performance less than one's best.

Perfectionism can contaminate Christian faith. The belief that one's spiritual condition is earned by good performance makes it impossible to accept God's grace joyfully. The person who comes to Christianity with a perfectionistic pattern is prone to fall into that trap.

There is, however, one area in life in which we should try to be perfect—in knowing and pleasing God. In that, though, we must keep an awareness that God loves us perfectly even though He knows that in this life we will remain imperfect.

Praise the Lord for His total and endless love that cannot be stopped by our self-defeating actions. Praise the Lord that we are created with the capacity to reach high and to dream beyond what we can reach. Praise the Lord for accepting us when we fail. Praise the Lord for freedom to become the best possible me.

10 | Freedom From Guilt:
A Proud Man Learns To Apologize

MACK RAN THE FEED store in his small prairie town. He was good at it. He understood soil and grain and animals; he understood customers and how to keep them coming back.

And the big man was strong. Hundred-pound bags of calf meal bounced around in his grip the way a person would fluff a pillow. A hearty, genial man of fifty-seven, he was admired locally for his courage, fairness, and business sense. His grass-roots view was "If everyone would work hard, be honest, and not change too fast, things would get a whole lot better real quick."

One of his personal traditions, "a foolish luxury" he called it, was to have each new pickup truck he bought painted his favorite color, cornsprout green. It was his way of celebrating the miracle of life.

People liked to be around him. He was such a good storyteller that he had become one of the main attraction in his crossroads town. Mack would toss bags on a two-wheeler and hustle from storeroom to loading dock with customers following along, back and forth like a herd of piglets, to hear the joke and watch him laugh when he hit the punch line. He'd laugh louder and longer while doing all that than anyone else could sitting still. It was fun.

Mack was just plain "Mack" to the people who knew him. He may have been C. R. Hayes at the courthouse, but newcomers were warned early not to ask Mack what C. R. stood for. They were also warned about Mack's sullen moods. Whenever he got grim and quiet, the hangers-around suddenly remembered things they had to do somewhere else.

Mack didn't get moody very often. The following episode is more typical.

One afternoon several of the regulars—Roy Mackson, B. D. Phillips, Bob Grimes—were hanging around when Conrad Fosse came in. Conrad was the local insurance and accounting expert and one of the few men in town who wore a tie outside of church.

Mack had been clowning around all morning, and when Conrad came in Mack was loaded for bear. He told one hilarious joke after another. Mack told a couple insurance salesman jokes, then one about a bookkeeper, and then he had some one-liners that had everyone aching from laughing. The jokes were all at Conrad's expense; but he laughed, too, although maybe not as much as the rest. I guess you would expect that, with him being the butt of every joke.

Mack was really "on," and Bob said it was funnier than one of those roasts you see on TV. That got Roy thinking because he always valued Bob's observations. It occurred to him that there usually was a cutting edge to Mack's remarks, and he thought, too, about a couple of things Mack said after Conrad left. "Ya know," he said, "I can't help wondering how that man lives so well. There can't be that much business in his line of work around here." And later he had said, "Ya know, Conrad has that funny nervous twitch about him, the sort of thing you see in somebody who has something they're trying to cover up."

So Roy had been thinking along those lines about Mack for a couple weeks when one day Mack dropped over to Roy's place and asked if he could tell him something personal. Mack was so subdued he didn't seem like the same person. Roy thought he saw honest fear in his eyes.

He told Roy about a dream he had had the night before. It was the first time Roy had ever heard him tell a story without being as fluent as a professional orator. The night before, Mack said, he had dreamed that he was in a fist fight with Conrad, that he had hit Conrad on the right side of his head, and that eyeballs popped out of Conrad, dozens of them, and they were rolling all over the floor like marbles. It frightened Mack enough to wake him up. Then he said that he was even more frightened when he realized that he understood perfectly well what the dream meant.

Mack explained that during his army days, a wild and reckless time of his life, he had hit a man viciously during a brawl. The man lost his sight in one eye. Mack felt so guilty that he vowed never to get physical again.

He kept that vow. In the place of violence, Mack learned to use jokes to make friends and to defuse tension and anger. But a more basic problem remained. He had not dealt with the sources of his anger. As a result, when Mack was with persons to whom he felt inferior, he used passive-aggressive behavior.

One form of this passive-aggressive behavior was telling hostile jokes. Mack was not really aware of the hostility in them. The fact that his audience laughed, and that usually the target of his jokes also laughed, covered up the fact that his humor was designed to insult and to dominate.

His other passive-aggressive behavior was dropping mysterious little comments that raised questions in people's minds. He had been only dimly aware that those comments were inappropriate.

He poured it all out. Saying it was painful to admit, he told Roy that he felt inferior to Conrad because Conrad had gone to college.

"I guess I'm a proud man," he said to Roy, "but I like to think that I run my business as good as he runs his, whether I went to college or not, and that I'm as honest as any man around. But I woke up this morning knowing that I haven't been honest at all. I haven't been honest with myself, and I haven't been honest in the way I talk about people."

He was right, of course, so Roy didn't say anything.

"So, now what do I do about it?" Mack asked.

"Mack, you've figured out so much on your own already why don't I just turn the question back to you?" Roy responded, "What do you think you need to do next?"

He laughed. "Unfortunately, I know what I need to do. I'm asking you because I don't want to do what I know I need to do. I'm shopping around for a better offer."

"What are you telling yourself?"

"I have to apologize."

He did. He started with Roy. He apologized for some wisecracks he had made about Roy that Roy hadn't thought of lately, although when Mack reminded him Roy realized he was still smoldering about them a little.

He apologized privately to Conrad and to a lot of others around the county. And then one day in the fall when there was a whole group hanging around, Mack said, "I've got a new story. It's kinda like a fable or parable or something. But it's a good one and I want you all to hear it.

"There was an old coyote, a fairly decent sort of coyote as those critters go. And he lived close to a real big prairie dog town. Now he could find good food easier than chasing those pesky prairie dogs, so he pretty much left them alone, except to tease them. What he would do would be to go down in the gully and pick up stones, the biggest ones he could get his mouth around, and bring them up and drop them down the prairie dog holes. He'd do that and then put his head down by the hole to listen and see if he could hear one of the little varmints down there scratching to dig around that big stone. And if he could, I swear, that old coyote would laugh.

"That went on for several years. Then one day our coyote tried to catch a pheasant, and that pheasant just slipped right out of the coyote's mouth. The pheasant didn't even act scared. In fact, the pheasant just laughed at the coyote and hopped along the ground teasing him. This made the coyote madder than anything, so he said, 'Where do you get off, you crummy pheasant, laughing at me?'

"'You can't hurt me, Mr. Coyote, you're so helpless you can't even take care of yourself. Your teeth are worn down to the gums. You're helpless now.'

"Sure enough, his teeth were gone, down to the gums, worn and broken down from lugging all those rocks. The pheasant just laughed at him.

"'Any fool could plainly see you weren't hurting anybody but yourself,' the pheasant taunted. 'I don't have to fly like an eagle to know that for every prairie dog hole you filled up they had fifteen other open holes. You haven't hurt anybody but yourself.' And the pheasant just sauntered away as carefree as can be while the coyote just stood there feeling stupid."

Mack chuckled. "You're looking at a rehabilitated coyote. You won't catch me biting rocks to drop on somebody's head again. I've done that to everyone of you good guys, but no more! I'm sorry."

"We hear you," said Bob. "We've all been coyotes, too."

"That's for you all to decide for yourselves. For right

now, let's raid the pop machine and see if there's enough Pepsis to go around."

Years ago, Mack's sinful lifestyle had caused him to make some serious mistakes—one was a fight in which he injured another man. That led to another mistake —the way he handled the situation. He did not deal with the root causes of his hostility when he gave up fighting physically. Instead, he continued to fight in another form. Because of his love for humor and his communication skills, he began using jokes as a way to attack. Along with that came subtle accusations. No one could have proved that Mack was doing anything vicious, but he hurt a lot of people.

Mack and Roy talked a lot about where that anger had come from. It was pretty easy to understand—Mack had taken a lot of cruel treatment as a child, and it had naturally created resentment in him. After Mack began to understand himself, he worked through his resentment by forgiving; and it made him a different person. He not only began to apologize immediately and extensively, but his love for people became very real. He learned to put his love into words and jokes that built people up rather than cut them down. As a result, spending time down at the feed store became even more special than before. There was something in the atmosphere that made a person feel young and healthy and vibrant and optimistic—like cornsprout green.

When we fail to forgive, almost inevitably our anger continues. Among those with gentle personalities, the anger is not expressed in direct fighting, but it often leaks out in passive-aggressive behavior. Passive-aggressive individuals find it difficult to recognize that behavior in themselves because they are unable to deal openly and directly with their anger. That is why passive-aggressive behavior became necessary for them in the first place. The passive-aggressive style is used to fool one's self.

Regardless of our personality styles, however, we should all pray regularly for God's help in learning about ourselves and our relationships. We each need close personal friends who will, when asked, tell us about our subtle sins and rough edges.

When we realize we have sinned against another person, we should ask God for direction about how to deal with it. Generally we will need to confess our sin to the other person and sincerely apologize. When possible, we should also make restitution, which is the process of putting things back the way they would have been had we not sinned.

An apology is an act of strength. It is evidence of maturity already attained and it helps build greater maturity. The important part of an apology is not what we say, but what we mean. The words of an apology tell the other person about our feelings, attitudes, and intentions; but it is how we live that counts. The following acronym, SORRY, will help us remember the five elements of a sincere apology:

SOON: The earlier we apologize, the better. That is difficult because it means changing our attitudes. But if we don't do it soon, we leave ourselves exposed to the cancer of resentment. The temptation to play the waiting game, hoping that the other person will apologize first or that we will forget about it, will be strong; but we must not give in to it.

OFFER: We must want to apologize. An apology that is pulled out of us is nothing more than hollow words.

REGRET: This means we wish we hadn't and we won't in the future. We cannot undo the past, but honest regret is a covenant to make future behavior better than past behavior.

RESTITUTION: We should do the best we can to restore the situation back to its original condition—to compensate for the damage we've done.

YOURSELF: The person who made the mess must clean it up. No one else should have to and, chances are, no one else will.

So then, being sorry means to "*S*oon *O*ffer *R*egret and *R*estitution *Y*ourself." It is easy to learn the right words. Simply say, "I'm sorry, will you forgive me?" or consider the following examples of apologies: "I spoke unkindly yesterday morning. I'm sorry." "Laughing at you awhile ago was inconsiderate. I wish I hadn't. Will you forgive me?" "I should have talked directly with you about the problem instead of with our neighbor. I apologize." Our words of apology should be spoken simply, specifically, and briefly, so that neither party is unduly embarrassed. And above all, we must avoid a "holier than thou" tone.

It is easy to know how to apologize, but not easy to actually do it. That is why we should ask God for His help. Sometimes we get annoyed with God for expecting us to apologize and then fail to ask Him to help us do it. God wants relationships between people to be restored by apologizing and forgiving; He will always help us with it.

It is worth the effort to apologize. Yes, it helps the other person, but our benefit is even greater. It frees us from guilt and shame about our own behavior and, usually, from their retaliation or from our fear of their retaliation. Our basic motivation for apologizing, however, should be out of obedience to God's wishes for us.

11 | Freedom From Prejudice:
Nora Loves "The Enemy"

GRANT AND NORA BOSTICK were an unusual couple. For example, how many people move from a small town in the Sun Belt to a city six hundred miles to the north when they retire? That's what Grant and Nora did. But they were special—filled with the enthusiasm and adventure of youth and the compassion and wisdom of age.

Grant volunteered to work for a year as an unpaid helper in a service center for homeless men. He was good at it, found it meaningful, and the one year had become two, three, four, five. Grant was hooked on helping and wanted to stay with the program another five years. Nora, involved with church and apartment complex activities of her own, was content.

But it was not to be. Grant was killed in a freak accident late one night. He had just started to cross a dark street when a car rounded the corner. Grant stepped quickly backward onto the sidewalk. The car did not hit him, but in stepping back he hit his heel on the curb, slipped, and fell, hitting the back of his head on a fire plug.

The police found him fifty-five minutes later,

slouched unconscious against a building half a block away. They saw no visible sign of injury and found no identification on him because his wallet had been stolen, so they thought he was a vagrant. They called an E-unit that delivered him to the detoxification unit of the city hospital thirty-five minutes later. Another thirty-eight minutes passed before he was given medical attention and his injury was discovered. By then he had been dead for twelve minutes. He might have been spared.

The initial shock for Nora was overwhelming. Her new friends were tremendously supportive and an amazing number of old friends rushed in for the funeral. Her pastor was a tower of strength and was quietly efficient in making arrangements behind the scenes. She drew on her deep reservoir of faith in God and knew His comfort.

The numbness had scarcely subsided when anger swept through her. In dealing with this, too, Nora had the help of her friends, Pastor Mason, and the Holy Spirit. Within a few weeks she was determinedly constructing a new pattern for the rest of her life. She knew things could never be the same, that there would always be a tremendous emptiness that Grant had filled, but she said, "I'm stubborn enough that I'm going to insist that God help me have a worthwhile life."

She had somehow found the capacity to forgive the unknown driver, the police and medical staff for their poor judgment and careless attitude, and the derelict who had taken Grant's wallet. She let go of her anger over what many had referred to as a streak of rotten luck. Pain was there twenty-four hours a day. Sometimes it was sharp and penetrating, as when she thought she heard his footsteps in the hall. And sometimes it was dull and aching, as when she thought ahead to silent meals and loneliness. But she also had determination and faith—until another event changed things.

Pastor Mason was the first to become aware of the new situation. He had just returned to his study after attending a breakfast prayer group when there was a light knock on his door. It was so cautious, so reluctant, that he was not sure it had even been a knock. Opening the door, he was surprised to see Matthew Chen, pastor of a Korean congregation nearby.

"This is a pleasant surprise. I didn't expect to see you again so soon after our breakfast, but it's very nice. Come on in."

Chen appeared distraught. He spoke quietly, but with urgency. "Forgive me, please, the intrusion. You deserve your time alone. But I must speak to you, and speak to you now. It's a matter of great personal importance."

"Quite all right. I don't have anything scheduled this morning. My time is yours."

"You spoke this morning about the tragic loss of Mr. Bostick. I knew him a little, but had not heard of his death. I have been gone for three weeks, to Korea, to visit churches that help support our work here. I was, of course, shocked this morning to hear the terrible news. But worse has happened."

Mason, puzzled, leaned forward and listened intently as his shaken friend continued.

"As I was driving from our breakfast to my church, I turned the corner where the accident must have happened. In a flash I remembered, for the first time, seeing our friend, Mr. Bostick, waiting to cross that street late one night about a month ago, a few days before my trip. The memory came to me so clearly it must be true. I must be the guilty driver."

Mason felt he was being strangled, the tentacles of this situation entwined around every member of his being, wrenching one part from another. He was dumfounded, unable to believe that there could be one more complicating feature to this awful chain of events. He scratched for words.

"You're not guilty—certainly, not guilty—Matthew, brother. The autopsy showed clearly that he had not been struck by the car. And you would not have been driving recklessly, I know that from having ridden with you. Please don't say you are guilty. You're not."

Chen was hunched at the edge of his chair, head down, eyes to the floor. He spoke in a hoarse whisper. "That doesn't help. I am responsible. I must do something."

"Responsible to God, and it is He who will tell you whether or not there is anything for you to do."

"I must confess to Mrs. Bostick."

"That is something to decide only after careful prayer. Could we pray together about this?" They did. After an hour or more of prayer and conversation and more prayer, Pastor Mason called Nora and asked if he could come over after lunch. She was eager to see him.

Pastor Mason went to Mrs. Bostick's alone. After a bit of small talk, her carefully explained the morning's events to Nora. She was silent as she listened, watching her pastor through teary eyes.

When he finished, she was breathing in short gasps and spoke with bitterness. "It was bad enough when all I knew was that it was a stranger. It's worse now. Oh-h-h—" Her voice faded away, and her body seemed to soak into the chair as if she were a teardrop being absorbed into the upholstery. She sat limply, staring into memory, peering back, back, back in time. Her eyes and lips grew narrow and hard.

Mason saw the sudden change, but did not understand it.

"Pastor, I should be alone now."

"I want to help if there is any way I can."

"You have been so kind and it has meant so much.

It still does. It was right for you to come and talk to me about this."

"Is there any way I can help—even if by just quietly staying here a little longer?"

"I should just be alone now."

"You'll be all right?"

"Yes."

"You'll call me if I can help?"

"I always do, don't I?" A smile flashed through her taut, grim expression and disappeared. Still worried, but a bit reassured, the pastor prayed and left.

He had not explained, as he thought he would, how much Reverend Chen wanted to visit her. He did not feel comfortable mentioning that for several weeks. When he did, Mrs. Bostick replied with certainty. "No, that's not necessary. Thoughtful of him, but not necessary. No."

Pastor Mason explained that Reverend Chen felt it very important to be able to speak with her. "Nora, I think you have an obligation to our brother in Christ, Matthew Chen, to help him find peace in his own heart about this," he said.

Nora almost shouted her reply. "No!"

The next morning, however, she called Pastor Mason and asked if he would bring Reverend Chen over. That morning Pastor Mason learned for the first time that Grant's and Nora's only child, Jim, had died in a Korean P.O.W. camp in 1951.

This began the healing of an old, smoldering resentment within Nora. "I knew I had this problem all along," she said. "Grant had worked it through in his own heart many years ago. I knew that because he had and I hadn't, he had an extra measure of freedom and joy that I never had."

A few months later, Nora again had a schedule of activity that kept her occupied, challenged and rewarded, despite the continuing ache of Grant's absence. But there was a new activity. Once a week she helped out in the day-care center at Midtown Community Korean Church. She learned a lot about love from the example of Reverend Chen, but she never did find out that his father and a brother had died in the war in 1951.

Nora thought she would never finish the process of forgiving those who had some connection with Grant's death. There were so many unidentified persons to forgive. She had been through a similar situation in 1951 and had not accomplished the forgiving process. Her anger toward the North Korean war machine had grown to a prejudice that irrationally included every human being in or connected with the Asian continent.

At times of tragedy, people frequently blame God when no specific human can be blamed. Nora had avoided that in 1951. She had avoided that error once again when Grant died—she had been able to forgive the nameless, faceless persons associated with the tragedy.

When one of those nameless, faceless persons was identified, however, especially when it tied in with the old prejudice, Nora had to begin the forgiving process all over again. Now it was harder because of her prejudice. But when she worked it through, not only was the present circumstance dealt with, but the old one was cleared up as well.

When we need to forgive, there is no risk, because forgiving always works to our benefit. It is not uncommon to benefit beyond our expectations. If we have not found this to be true in our experiences with God, we should ask Him to teach us about His love for us and to show us what we need to forgive. He will reveal the problem areas in our lives and lovingly create in us a new spirit, a new life, and His love.

12 | Freedom From Anger Toward God:
How Larry Found a Friend

LARRY BURNSIDE WAS the best sales representative any company could hope for. He worked hard and enthusiastically, and he had mastered the art of positive human relations. Beth, his wife, listened with admiration one Saturday morning as Larry talked on the phone to a customer. She knew that before he was finished, the customer would be almost at the point of thanking Larry for the price increases he was announcing. Beth said that Larry could make anyone deliriously happy while telling them bad news. Despite the exaggeration, there was no question that Larry could be very persuasive, while at the same time remaining honest and fair.

Beth knew a side of Larry the others didn't know. It grated on her at times, as it did now, that he could be so accommodating to others and yet so inflexible about some of her requests, one in particular.

Larry hung up the phone and, with a sigh of dread, said, "We might as well get that conversation finished up."

"I don't think I'm asking for very much. All I'm asking is that you go to church with me tomorrow and once in a while in the future. You don't have to go all the time and you don't have to get involved in everything that's going on, but I want you to come once in a while. I don't think that's much to ask."

"A guy in sales, like me, if he goes just once in a while, people think he's only showing up because he wants to meet people he can sell things to. I'm not a phony and I don't want people thinking I'm one. That wouldn't be fair to you."

"And that's another glib excuse. You have the perfect line for everything that comes up, and your line always makes sense on the surface. But that doesn't take away from the fact that you need to be in church, for the right reasons, no matter what anyone else might think."

"You know I'm a Christian. I just worship in my own way. That means just as much."

Beth wanted to disagree, but before she spoke they both heard a car door slam and saw Larry's father walking briskly toward the front door.

Larry snatched a magazine from the coffee table and hurled it in the general direction of the wastebasket across the room. "Aw, sheesh! Why does he have to show up on Saturday?"

When the doorbell rang, Larry could picture his father impatiently jabbing it repeatedly, shifting from foot to foot and scowling at the delay. Larry dawdled on the way to the door.

"Hi, dad. Something real urgent?"

"No, I just happened to be in the neighborhood and thought I'd drop by and say hello."

"Come on in."

They sat in the living room, eyeing each other cautiously.

"The real-estate market is going to get good again fast, Larry. It's the right time for you to get in the business. Your office-machine stuff is going to go right down the tubes with all this foreign competition. Real estate will always be good, Larry, because they aren't making any more of it. The Japanese aren't going to start exporting land, that's for sure!"

Larry had heard his father's pitch a hundred times, and he gave him his conventional response. "Dad, I'm doing something I like, I'm doing it well, and it's real comfortable for me. I like it, my customers like me, and my company likes me. I think I'm where I belong."

Like two bull elk performing a mating-season ritual, the younger and the older each testing the other's defense of his territory, Larry and his dad continued to spar.

"Here's an article from a trade journal, Larry. It talks about the coming shake out in the office-machine industry. There are a lot of companies that just aren't going to survive. This article names names. Look here, where I've circled the names of a couple of your products. It's a good time to get out of what *you're* doing and into what *I'm* doing."

"Dad, we've talked about that before, and believe me, I'm flattered to have you want me in business with you. It just isn't what's right for me."

"Read the article, Larry. Read it and tell me what you think then."

Larry caught himself wishing his dad would speak with invitation instead of command, but said nothing and tried to hide his impatience.

"I've got to be running along, Larry. I've got a big deal cooking. Who says you can't make money in this economy? I'll talk to you later." He was quickly gone.

Larry clenched the article tightly, but not out of affection. He paced a couple of laps around the coffee table as Beth watched anxiously.

"He's always leaning on me! Always pushing! Always telling me how to run my life!"

Beth stood silently, aching to be able to heal the hurt she knew Larry had on these occasions. "I wish I knew what to do, Larry. I wish I knew."

Beth went to church alone the next day and waited until the following Thursday, after they had finished a candlelit supper, to approach the subject of church attendance again. Larry exploded.

"Don't start in on me about that! I've warned you about it before. Get off my back, you nag!"

"Nag?" Beth yelled. "Nag? Me, a nag?" Tears filled her eyes. Her mind swirled as she tried to figure out how to respond.

"You're on my back constantly, pounding away at me to go to church with you. Well, I won't." He stood up.

"You're no Christian," she snarled at him. "And you're not man enough to be a husband if you can't do any better than have a tantrum when your wife makes a reasonable request!" She stomped into the kitchen.

He almost knocked over the table following her. She whirled and said, "Go away, leave me alone. Stay out of here."

"It's my house. I belong here."

"Then I'll leave." She moved away, turning toward the bedroom.

He grabbed her arm and jerked her around to face him. His left hand pressed her shoulder, and he raised his right hand to slap her.

He froze in this position, and Beth saw tears in his eyes as he slowly lowered both arms to his sides. He turned and walked away, sobbing. There was an uneasy, silent cease-fire that evening and they both slept fitfully at opposite edges of their king-sized bed.

The next day Larry was able to get himself a short appointment with Dr. Floyd Bell, an industrial psychologist who specialized in career management. Larry had consulted him before for help with vocational decisions.

"Doc, I was planning to come in and hide my real problem behind a smoke screen of questions about my career; but since you were good enough to work me into your schedule today, let me just lay it on the line and get on with it. The problem is, I came within an inch of hitting my wife last night, and it scares the breath out of me."

In the process of sketching in the background information, Larry's anger toward his father was revealed. Larry denied there was any significance in that.

"So I am bugged at my dad. Big deal! I just came for some quick advice about my wife, I don't need a bunch of Freudian fraud!"

"That's putting it in pretty harsh terms, Larry, but I agree that we don't need Freud to understand this. Let me ask you a question. Do you suppose there might be a connection between your frustration with your dad and your stubbornness, to the point of explosiveness, about not going to church?"

"No!"

"You say that so quickly that I wonder whether you have had time to think about it."

"Okay, you have something up your sleeve so just lay it on me. What's your theory?"

"Larry, as you know, God is often referred to as our heavenly Father. Do you think you might be angry with God because you're angry with your earthly father?"

"Aw! Sheesh! If I wanted religion I could just as well have gone to church!"

"But you came here knowing that my Christian faith is very important to me, and that I will offer you the best of what I can offer. If I find you starving, I'm going to give you food whether you want it or not. I'm always going to give you what you need, even though it may not be what you want."

Larry rubbed his face in both hands, sighed, and leaned back in his chair. "I see your point. I don't like it, but you're probably right." He leaned forward facing Bell squarely. "Okay, Dr. Bullseye, now that I know that, what do I do about it?"

They looked at each other with respect. "You need someone to help you meet both those fathers."

"Who?"

"If I remember correctly, you don't have a brother do you, Larry?"

"No." He paused, smiled, and continued. "I had a brother in my imagination."

"What was he like?"

"Well, he was everything you could design into a brother: he would stick up for me; he liked me; he could answer all my questions; and we did things together. Whenever I thought about him being around, I felt very safe. It was pretty real to me."

"He sounds a lot like your heavenly brother."

"Who?"

"When our relationship with God is restored through belief in His Son, we become a son or daughter of God. Jesus, the Son of God, becomes our spiritual brother. Jesus is our advocate to the Father, or, to use your terms, He sticks up for us. For that reason we need not fear the Father and we can begin enjoying the special benefits of our relationship with God.

"Then," Bell went on, "we are able to benefit from the comfort and counsel of the Holy Spirit and from the companionship of Christ within us, and we discover that God really can be trusted. As we begin to understand that God really does love us and that He really does want us to be joyous in this life, we are able to drop the barriers we have put up between us and others."

Larry was puzzled. "If I'm following you, you're saying that I don't trust God because He reminds me of my dad, but that I need God's help in order to get along better with my dad. Which came first, the chicken or the egg?"

"We don't need to understand where it started."

"But it looks like it's going around and around in circles. How do I break this cycle?"

"Your heavenly brother helps you with that."

"Okay, I see that now," he said impatiently, "but who helps me get through to my dad?"

"At that point there is a new Larry. That Larry can do it because that Larry will want to do it. And that Larry will allow God to work through him, something that this Larry has not permitted. The new Larry will be able to forgive his father."

"Will I need to forgive God, too?"

"No, we never have occasion to forgive God because God is never unjust. It may seem like it to us, as it has to you sometimes, but God is always totally loving to us. When we feel anger toward God we should report that to Him, ask Him to help us understand it, and submit to His authority in our lives."

Larry was silent for several minutes and then said, "It makes sense when you explain it all to me this way. I'll think about it."

He did, and several weeks later he committed himself to full cognitive and operational belief in God, through His Son Jesus Christ, and the Holy Spirit guided Larry into reconciliation with Beth and with his father.

There were a lot of things Larry wanted to talk to his dad about. He wanted to apologize, to forgive his dad's mistakes, to share hurts and fears, and to begin getting acquainted and having fun with him. The following pointers that Dr. Bell gave Larry will also be helpful for us:

1. Determine if we really should talk with the other person about these things. Prayer is essential in

making this decision, and talking with a trusted Christian friend can also be very valuable.

2. Rehearse the conversation of forgiving. There are three benefits from this: practicing what we are going to say will make it easier to actually say it; as we practice we will learn a lot about ourselves, our behavior, and about the other person; and our attitudes may begin to change. Methods of rehearsal include:

a. Fantasy. Imagine that we are forgiving the other person. Picture it and hear it in our minds the way we want it to happen, with the conversation coming out the way we would like it to come out.

b. With an empty chair. Sit facing another chair and imagine the other person is in it. Say the things we would like to say to that person. Think about how the person might feel and anticipate his or her response. This is a vivid way of coming to a complete understanding of the situation and to an understanding of our attitudes about it as well.

c. With a friend. Find someone who understands our circumstances, cares about us, and who has the emotional energy to invest in helping us. Ask that person to pretend to be the other person. Say to the role player what we would like to say to the "real" person and let the role player respond. Keep this simulation realistic and positive. Be open to gaining new understandings.

3. Tell the other person we want to talk, face-to-face if we can. Don't make a big production out of setting this up. When we do talk, make it easy for the other person. Keep anger out of it, because that will only raise defensiveness. Remind ourselves that our forgiving is only possible because of God's work in us.

4. Apologize.

5. Listen for the following clues:

a. those that reveal we are exaggerating or di-
minishing the importance of what happened.

b. those that give us greater insight into our
sins against the person.

c. those that indicate we have accepted the person. (We must accept the person even though we
cannot accept that person's behavior.)

6. Report how the person's behavior affected us.
Pretend to be a newscaster who is stating facts, rather
than a critic who is evaluating the other person. For
example, say, "When you scoffed at my opinion in front
of that group, it really embarrassed me; I felt about two
inches tall," instead of, "What kind of person are you,
to put me down that way? I haven't heard a remark that
immature since grade school!"

We may wish to say that both of us are responsible
for what happened, but we should not obscure the
other person's responsibility by overemphasizing our
own, and we should not go into detail about assigning
blame. For example, say, "Some of the flippant remarks
I was making about people must have made it easy for
you to say what you said."

7. Make a statement of forgiving. If it is proper for
us to talk to the person, then it is proper for us to be
precise and direct. Simply say, "I forgive you." We don't
have to use those exact words, but they are hard to beat
for being brief and easy to understand. They may be
hard for the other person to believe, but that's not our
problem. We should also explain why we wanted to tell
them this.

8. Affirm the other person as a person. Give the
message "You are worthwhile." If we can't say that with
no strings attached, we haven't yet forgiven the person.

Over a period of many months, Larry and his dad
had many discussions, good times, and congenial ar-
guments. And eventually they had occasions of deep
personal sharing and prayer. One day over lunch

Larry's father said, "I thought for years that I ought to have a partner. Maybe I'm not the kind of guy who is suited for having a partner. I thought I might go talk to that friend of yours, the businessman shrink, Bell. Would he take on an old duffer like me as a client?"

Larry grinned. "That's progressive thinking. Anybody who thinks like that is not a duffer. As far as I'm concerned, that proves you don't need him; so let me ask you this: Could a progressive guy like you use a partner like me?"

He could.

Larry needed to understand the connection between his anger toward his father and his attempts to avoid God. But understanding was not enough. He also needed to spend time with his natural father so they could get acquainted, learn to understand one another, and eventually apologize and forgive one another. Once Larry accepted Christ's offer to intercede on his behalf with the heavenly Father, God could begin the process of reconciling Larry with the other important persons in his life. Larry moved from his therapeutic relationship with Floyd Bell to a personal relationship with Christ and forgiveness from God. From his personal relationship with Christ, Larry moved to a trusting relationship with God. And from trusting God, Larry moved to friendship with Beth and his father.

We are each created with a unique combination of gifts and interests, and wanting to identify them and find fulfillment in them is normal and desirable; but going our own way never leads to that result, only living in partnership with God does.

God can handle our anger toward Him; we cannot. God wants us; we need Him.

When we are angry with God, we should tell Him we are angry and, through that, discover that He continues to love us anyway. We should search our attitudes and see if there are any barriers between us and

God. If there are, we cannot possibly be functioning at our best in our relationships with others, and we cannot possibly be as content within ourselves as we could be. When we tell God we are angry with Him, He will help us understand our feelings. Then we will be able to resolve our anger and begin to enjoy the full benefit of God's overwhelming love for us.

13 | Freedom From Worry About Tomorrow's Hurts:
Anna's Rebellious Child

LIFE HAD NEVER BEEN easy for Anna, but by age fifty-five she had gained widespread recognition and respect in her small town. She had taken a warm personal interest in several thousand grade school music students to whom she had been more than teacher. She was active in all civic activities that had anything to do with music, was a benevolent queen bee in her church groups, and was held up to the youth of the community as "the way you ought to turn out someday."

She was a pleasant, giving person, and was so devoted to her teaching that no one thought it out of the ordinary when this woman, whose only child had moved away many years ago, enrolled in a course in parenting skills. "I am parent to five hundred and sixty children a week," she had said.

And when this conservative, dedicated, model citizen had said once, "I'd like to be buried in white, to meet Jesus looking clean," no one thought anything about it. The general public saw her professional competence and her genuine love for children. Adults gave her respect, but felt they didn't know her. Kids felt they knew her and they loved her.

No one suspected her agonizing self-loathing, her resentment and self-pity, nor the shrew-like demands she made on her thirty-year-old daughter, Rosalee Webster. Nor did they know that Anna regarded herself as a deceiver and intensely feared that she would no longer be able to keep up the deception.

Sitting in her prim, somewhat old-fashioned living room, surrounded by dozens of pictures of Rosalee, framed letters from former students, and cross-stitched mottoes, Anna felt ugly and dirty. She sat curled into a wing-backed overstuffed chair, idly picking at the edge of a crocheted antimacassar. She was concentrating on self-pity.

"I quit teaching so I could offer Rosalee more during her crucial adolescent years. I was lucky to get back in the system and hold my job. She doesn't know what I go through now so that I could provide better for her back then. I could be retired now. She doesn't know what I went through, as a single parent, raising her back in those days when there weren't all the programs and conveniences there are now."

Anna's husband, Ned Mayfield, was killed in a mine accident in Eastern Kentucky when Rosalee was one month old. Anna moved north for a better salary and remained. Rosalee grew up, attended college, married and divorced, lived with Anna for two years, and then moved to New York City. Of all the adjustments in Anna's life, Rosalee's last move had been the most traumatic.

"After all I'd done for her, she walked out on me. It isn't fair. Now as I'm getting older and I'm going to need her more, she's gone. It isn't fair."

She was startled by the postman's footsteps on the front porch and, through the thin ruffled covering over the oval window of the dark oak front door, saw him approach the mail slot. A slender blue envelope fell inside beside the door. Anna didn't move, but studied the envelope from her chair. Day after day for a year she had hoped for a letter from Rosalee; none had come. Could this be a letter from Rosalee? She wanted it to be, hoped it was, but preferred the hope to disappointment. Wearily she rose, retrieved the letter, and began to tremble when she saw Rosalee's initials. She took a deep breath and tore it open.

She gasped. Rosalee was coming to visit! Rosalee wrote, "Mama, there are too many things we haven't said to each other over the years. I'm coming so I can listen, because I want to know who you are, who you really are, like you've never let me know you before."

Anna sat down to read the letter again. She was afraid.

A few weeks later Rosalee came. Anna was relieved to see her looking healthy and was pleased with Rosalee's enthusiasm about her career; but the uncertainty about the conversations Rosalee wanted hung heavily and precariously over both of them. They knew they had a basic love for one another, but that they had not begun to express it freely. They both wanted to.

After supper on the second day of Rosalee's visit, mother and daughter sat in the living room, Anna curled in her chair, and Rosalee slouched comfortably on the sofa. They were both tense, knowing the time for serious conversation had come.

Rosalee spoke cautiously. "Mama, you've done so much for me over the years, I can't begin to name it all. But there are other things that have hurt me as much as all of those things have helped me. I just can't go on feeling anger about that. I've got to get rid of that anger, and I think the way to do it—the way that's right for both you and me—is for us to talk about it. Maybe I feel that I don't know you because of my resentment."

Anna stroked her carefully dyed blue-gray hair. "I tried, Rosalee, and I'm not ready to quit trying. Say whatever you have to say."

"Mama, I just want to know who you are. I feel like I don't know you any better than any of the other people in town. I was in your classes, so I know the professional you. I saw you do a hundred things in public and at church, so I know that part, too. But you haven't given me anything of yourself that's different than what you've given to audiences. I want that from you, and I need that from you. Just tell me who you are."

Tears streamed down Anna's face. "I've given you my best, Rosalee. I've given you the part of me that's worthwhile. I've only wanted you to see the part of me that is worth imitating. That's not a very big part of me. There is so much of me that is so rotten and so wrong and so dirty that I don't want you to see it. You can't blame me for that. I've only wanted you to have the part of me that's good."

"Mama, with me it's different! I'm your daughter! If you don't let me know all of you, then I'm not really your daughter, I'm just another person! Whatever it is, I can try to understand it, and I can learn to love you, every bit of you. But I don't think I can love *any* of you if I don't know *all* of you. Mama, you've just got to tell me about all of you."

"But I can't. I can't tell you some things because, well, they're just too terrible."

"I don't believe that. Whatever you might tell me, it can't be as terrible as not knowing you. Mama, do you know how terrible *that* is?"

They both cried because they knew exactly how terrible that was. They cried from the exhaustion of living with the distance between them. They cried in anticipation of the joy that could be theirs when they would no longer be teacher and child, but would in fact be mother and daughter. Rosalee could see her mother searching for words and for the courage to say them. Anna struggled to begin, and Rosalee patiently waited.

Finally, Anna began to speak in a rasping, faltering

voice. "Your father—your father and I—uh—well, we weren't married. Oh, when you were *born,* yes! But, not very long before." She paused and then burst out, almost shouting, and with no effort to hold in her sobbing, "I'm so ashamed!"

Rosalee knelt beside the chair and stroked her mother's arm, eager to hug her, but it wasn't possible. "Don't be, Mama. I know about it. I've known it for a long time—known it forever, it seems like. Grandma told me that years ago. About me." She hesitated, then went on softly. "About you, too. That you and me are alike as far as that goes."

Anna was stunned. Numbness swept over her in a wave. So Rosalee knew; she had always known! And it didn't matter to her. It had never mattered—none of it!

After the numbness came tingling warmth. She heard the healing words again. "Mama, it's okay. I love you. I don't care what happened way back then. I just want to *know you.* "

Anna peered through watery eyes to see Rosalee leaning forward, both arms outstretched. As Rosalee repeated, "I love you, Mama," Anna rose and they embraced.

The hugging and crying lasted a long time, and the conversation even longer. They confessed to one another. They learned about each other's fear and shame. They began to understand one another and, with that, to forgive, and then to celebrate the forgiving.

During this process Anna learned an important lesson about God. Anna reasoned, "If I can accept an imperfect Rosalee, why should not God, whose ability to accept is unlimited, accept me? He will. He has!"

The realization of God's love for her broke through to a new level of understanding for Anna! She prayed, "Dear Lord, you do love me, don't you! You do! You *have* forgiven me—you did so long ago, didn't you?

Long ago, yes, and thank you. I *am* your child, and I love you, as I have told you thousands of times; but now I know that you love me—really do—and that my sins *are* covered—fully covered, because of the death of your Son, Jesus Christ, and His miraculous resurrection. You've given me life, and I know it. I can feel it even now. Thank you. Thank you. Thank you!"

Anna had, for years, known that God had forgiven her for her past. She had understood it; she had received it; but she had never accepted it.

When she talked about it later to her pastor, he explained it to her this way: "Anna, it is just as though you had ordered a new dress from a mail-order place. The United Parcel driver brought the package to your door. You signed for it and brought the package inside. You understood exactly what was in there. You had received it. But then you put the package aside, unopened. You had not really accepted what you had received. By not taking full possession of it, by not using the rights of ownership, by not wearing that dress, you didn't get any benefit from it. It was there, but it did not change your wardrobe—it could have, but you didn't let it. We know that you have received God's forgiveness because you have confessed your sins. As 1 John 1:9 says, 'If we confess our sins, he is faithful and just and will forgive us our sins and purify us from all unrighteousness.' You have received forgiveness; now you must accept it."

A few weeks later Anna noticed she was not thinking very often about her past sins. She would occasionally, but less and less frequently. And her feelings of guilt and shame were gone. She had *accepted* God's forgiveness.

Anna thinks of her relationships with God and with Rosalee as friendships—pure and fun and comfortable. The healing, brought by confessing and forgiving, has endured. Her joy shall be forever.

When we sin we should confess to God and repent promptly and honestly—once. Anna received God's forgiveness the first time she asked; she accepted it years later.

Then she learned to rest in God's love. In doing that she drew strength that took her on to greater service, joy, and contentment.

With her self-condemnation gone, she was free to develop a new kind of relationship with her daughter. When Anna accepted herself, it became possible for her to let her daughter accept her.

God's forgiveness opens the door to free and full relationships with others. To receive it we must honestly confess and repent. God delivers forgiveness promptly. We can ignore it, or we can claim it, use it, and begin living as though we had never been guilty. In Christ we are new creatures. Hallelujah!

14 | Our Forgiving of Others:
License or Limits?

FORGIVING IS SOMETHING we must always do as part of our response to injustice. We may need to do it over and over. We do not always need to talk with the other person about the forgiving, although we may, as illustrated in chapter 12 about Larry and his dad.

We should never give others the impression that our forgiving gives the person permission to take advantage of us. We have a responsibility to help others do what is right and avoid doing what is wrong. Forgiving is not issuing a license for others to hurt us. We are responsible for putting limits on what we allow others to do to us.

When we forgive we release our claim against the person who hurt us. Our goal is reconciliation—we are reconciled with God; we are reconciled with the offending person; and ideally, that person is eventually reconciled with God. In fact, part of our motivation for forgiving comes from our desire that the relationship continues.

Even though we release the person from our claim against him or her, it is not within our power to release the person from God's claim on him or her; nor does it release that person from responsibility under civil law, as seen in chapter 7 about Tom and his ex-wife, Bette. Tom forgave; Bette continued to sin; Tom continued to forgive. But Bette's sins finally came to the point that society recognized her injustices against the children and took corrective action. While regrettable—it was agonizing to Tom and the children as well as devastating to Bette—it was the proper consequence for her improper behavior.

It would have been wrong for Tom to have remained silent about Bette's destructive course. Before he accepted Christ, his remarks were hostile and degrading; after becoming a believer, he continued to protest her destructiveness, but in a style of love. Even though he was doing the right things and doing them well, they were ineffective; Bette used the freedom God gives us, but in the wrong way.

Part of God's plan since the earliest days has been for believers to lovingly confront one another. "Do not hate your brother in your heart. Rebuke your neighbor frankly so you will not share in his guilt" (Lev. 19:17). "Have nothing to do with the fruitless deeds of darkness, but rather expose them" (Eph. 5:11). "Instead, speaking the truth in love, we will in all things grow up into him who is the Head, that is, Christ" (Eph. 4:15). "And we urge you, brothers, warn those who are idle, encourage the timid, help the weak, be patient with everyone. Make sure that nobody pays back wrong for wrong, but always try to be kind to each other and to everyone else" (1 Thess. 5:14–15).

Reproof of our sins is also given to us by ministers (Mic. 3:8; Jer. 44:4; Ezek. 3:17) and by the Bible (Ps. 19:7–11; 2 Tim. 3:16). We should not be negligent in picking up our share of this task with others, however.

Our forgiving of others represents the forgiveness available to them from God; by seeing Christ in us, others will better understand the meaning of atonement.

How we handle our claims against others is one of the most important influences in shaping how others will respond to God's claim on them. If we are picky and demanding, the image of God others see in us is a disagreeable one. If we are generous and merciful, others see that image of God, which is so much more accurate. This puts a lot of responsibility on us. As we think of that, it should encourage us to maintain our fellowship with God so that we really do live in partnership with Him.

We have a stewardship responsibility to keep ourselves healthy physically and emotionally. If we don't, we cannot carry out our obligations to God, to family, to employer, or to others. With this in mind, we put limits on the extent to which we allow others to abuse us. Doing right will mean abuse part of the time; that goes with the turf. But inviting abuse or failing to deal with it is wrong.

May we all pray for God to teach us how to speak out effectively against injustice. May we have the patience to forgive and forgive, the courage to protest evil in every form in which it comes, and may we do all that we do with Christ-like love, which is a gift from our heavenly Father.

15 | Learning If I Need To Forgive

SOMETIMES THE INJUSTICE done to us is so obvi-
ous we can easily identify it and clearly understand the
necessity of forgiving whoever is responsible. At other
times it may not be easy to identify who hurt us or to
determine whether or not we have already forgiven.

There is only one sure way to know those things—
ask God to teach us. One way to do that is to pray along
these lines: "Lord, help me become aware of the things I
need to learn about myself (or this situation or my relationship with that person). Give me the understanding I need so that I can be obedient to your principles for this situation." This is specific enough, yet
does not try to compete with God's sovereignty by at-
tempting to tell Him what to do. In doing this we are
acting on James 1:5, "If any of you lacks wisdom, he
should ask God, who gives generously to all without
finding fault, and it will be given to him." God is always
willing to teach us what we need to know to become
more obedient to His will. In my experience as a counselor, every person who has honestly prayed this over a
period of a week or two has been led to understand
things that needed to be understood for that person's
own progress and benefit.

The situation of a young woman comes to mind. She was experiencing fear of people, irritability with her husband, and symptoms of depression. Her father had been unstable in family leadership, and she felt considerably distant from him. Conventional psychological thought pointed to that relationship as the primary focus for our attention. So I asked her to use her strong Christian faith in a practical way and to pray daily, asking God to reveal the things she needed to learn about her relationship with her father. The goal was for her to understand and desire to do whatever needed to be done to heal and restore her relationship with her father. Almost as an afterthought, I suggested that she pray the same prayer in regard to her relationship with her mother.

She prayed for this twice daily for two weeks. When I saw her again at the end of that time, I asked her what she had learned about her relationship with her father. She said she had not thought very much about her father and had no new ideas. Puzzled (and, frankly, somewhat disappointed that there had been no dramatic breakthrough), I asked her what else had happened during that period of time.

"Oh!" she exclaimed. "The funniest thing! For the last week I have been thinking about my mother almost all the time and I have realized a lot of things I had never thought of before. You know, I thought my father was the problem, but I realize now that it really is my relationship with my mother that is the bigger problem—and it isn't her, it's me."

She went on to describe several very important things she had needed to understand about her relationship with her mother and what she needed to do about those. The following week she was able to spend some time with her mother. She confessed to God her hardness of heart toward her mother, repented, and forgave her mother for the sins she had unintentionally and unknowingly committed against her.

God knows what we need to learn. He is the perfect counselor, the perfect teacher. He is efficient. (This is why I no longer engage in individual counseling. To the extent that my humanness allows, I work as co-therapist with God, and what a privilege that is!)

Prayer is the most important avenue to growth and development. God responds to our prayers and speaks to us as we thoughtfully inventory our attitudes and experiences. The questions on the list below will help make us aware of our need to forgive someone. Any of these items can be related to other matters; but when we become aware of these attitudes or actions in our-selves, we should determine if, perhaps, we have been hurt by someone and have neglected to forgive that person for the offense.

1. Do I think often about the hurt? (This is the seedbed for resentment.)

2. When I think about the hurt, do I have strong feelings of anger?

3. Do I imagine difficulty or injury coming to the person who hurt me?

4. Do I avoid the person or not communicate with him or her when it would be easy for me to do so?

5. Do I have physical symptoms of tension, tight-ness, stomach disorder, or insomnia?

6. Am I irritable? Do I easily get angry about little things?

7. Do I indirectly attack the other person? This might take the form of hostile humor, spreading half-true stories, trying to turn children or others against that person, failing to cooperate or be supportive, or any of hundreds of other forms of passive-aggressive behavior.

8. Do I attack the person directly through harsh insults, sarcasm, physical attack, withholding child-support payments, or some other form of direct attack?

9. Am I highly critical of myself? Am I discontented with life, self-demanding, self-condemning, or generally dissatisfied with myself?

If our answers to items 7 or 8 above, and perhaps others, are yes, it is our responsibility to change our behavior and to apologize for our sins against the other person as well as to forgive. In every instance when we forgive someone else, we need to pray that God will make us aware of our sins against the other person. We must also pray for humility and charity in our relationships.

These two methods, prayer and thoughtful personal inventory accompanied by prayer, will help us learn what we need to know about our need to forgive. If possible, we should talk with a sensible, reliable Christian friend or counselor during this process.

When we genuinely seek to know the truth, God will teach us what we need to know at that point in time. What we learn may not be in the area in which we expected it to be, but it will be what we need to know. *God is the perfect friend and teacher.*

At times it may seem that no answer is coming. If we have prayed honestly a number of times, perhaps for a couple of weeks, for information in a particular area and no answer seems to come, it is likely we do not need that particular information at that particular time. We may accept that as an indication the situation is properly taken care of. At that point we should thank God that forgiving has taken place and assume there is no need for further action on our part. If God wants us to know something we have sincerely inquired about, He will let us know. There is only one way our loving Lord works—in our best interest.

God is very pleased to respond to our requests to learn how to live according to His plan. We should seek God's direction so we can move into the joyful life He wants us to have.

16 | Summary of How To Forgive

IN PREVIOUS CHAPTERS general principles about forgiving were described and illustrated. This chapter summarizes the practices derived from the principles.

First of all, remember there is no one way in which forgiving takes place. This chapter will present pieces of the process in the order in which they often occur, but this should not, by any means, be interpreted as a rigid formula.

God must participate in the forgiving process, and He will always do it in the pattern that is best for us. The purpose of this summary is to facilitate thoughtful and prayerful exploration of various areas of life.

Prayer is an essential part of the forgiving process. A prayer of commitment indicating our desire to learn the forgiving process and the forgiver's lifestyle is a good place to begin. Here is such a prayer:

> Heavenly Father, forgiveness is something you have freely given me. I don't understand forgiveness or why you have forgiven me, but I thank you for it. You want me to forgive others, but it is so hard because it seems unfair that I must forgive when I have been mistreated. Yet I will, with your

help. Teach me how. Give me the courage to do what you show me I should do and the ability to proceed with your wisdom and love flowing through me. Amen

Now, we shall consider the steps in the process.

0. The low point is zero. Here we are bound by resentment and controlled by how we feel about the offense and by what we do in response to it.

1. Receive God's forgiveness. Change begins with a proper relationship with God, which begins when we confess and repent of our sins. Receiving forgiveness and forgiving others go hand in hand. This is shown in the Lord's Prayer (Matt. 6:12; Luke 11:4) and in Christ's words, "For if you forgive men when they sin against you, your heavenly Father will also forgive you. But if you do not forgive men their sins, your Father will not forgive your sins" (Matt. 6:14–15).

This does not mean that our salvation is contingent on our having forgiven all who have hurt us. We cannot forgive until we have God living within us and until we have His participation in the forgiving process. But these verses definitely mean that if we neglect to forgive others, we are separated from full fellowship with God.

For some persons, like Anna, receiving God's forgiveness is difficult. Writing a prayer of thankfulness that celebrates God's forgiveness often makes it easier to receive that forgiveness. Here is a composite prayer written by two friends who have received, with thankfulness, God's forgiveness:

> Dear Father, Almighty God, thank you! You have forgiven my sins! For nearly a year my life has been chaos and confusion. You had not forsaken me, but I had separated myself from you. In your Word you say that if we confess our sins, you are faithful and just to cleanse us. I have claimed this verse, have asked for your forgiveness in Jesus'

name, and with my heart and mind opened up to receive what you have promised, I have been forgiven!

Thank you for this forgiveness, so free for all of us. Thank you for the assurance that my sins are forgiven and that you have removed them from me as far as the east is from the west.

You have given me joy overflowing and a heart filled with gratitude. Help me to grow, to mature in my devotion to you, to serve others. In Christ's name I rejoice in new life and pray this with the assurance of your love. Amen

Those who have written similar prayers have found, with few exceptions, that the experience is very valuable to them, often in unexpected ways.

2. Quit hurting the other person. Forgiving is the opposite of vengeance; we cannot have both. If we have chosen to forgive, we must quit doing things that are contrary to forgiving.

3. Decide we are willing to want to apologize and to forgive. When forgiving seems impossible, we should remember that God will help us and that He is satisfied when we start wherever we are.

We may begin at the point where we don't even want to forgive, but in obedience to God's commands, we are *willing to want* to apologize and forgive. Although this is a small step, it is probably the most difficult one to make. It is an essential step because it is a deliberate act of the will to be obedient to God's commands.

Prayer at this point emphasizes our willingness to learn and to allow our attitudes to be shaped by the Holy Spirit. Here is a prayer asking for that:

Heavenly Father, you ask me to forgive others. It seems so hard, and I've tried so often and failed. When I consider your forgiveness to me, whatever forgiving I might be able to do seems so paltry and incomplete. I can't do it on my own. Help me let go of the resentments and jealousies that seem so important to me. Teach me to allow the love you have for me to flow through me to others so that relationships are restored and your will is done. Amen

4. Begin to want to apologize and forgive. Moving to this point is partly the result of our willful obedience and partly God's response to that obedience. God gives us an infusion of His love that begins to change our attitude.

5. Make amends for sins against the other person. This means apologizing and making restitution, to the extent possible, for what we have done.

6. Determine if talking to the other person about the forgiving is necessary.

7. Forgive. During this process there is a point at which, through an act of the will, we let go of the claims against the other person. We may be aware of it when we do this, but the awareness is not necessary. The act of the will to release the claim is necessary.

Included in this, I believe, is a covenant before God to serve that other person in whatever way is appropriate. This service may not involve us directly with that person—we may never speak to them or do anything directly with them—but we would be willing to do so. Our attitudes and behavior change from seeking justice to being willing to serve the person who hurt us.

8. Claim forgiveness and forgiving. Close the incident. A prayer of thanksgiving for this occasion is appropriate. Here is a prayer of celebration:

Lord, miracles are happening! You have forgiven me, and you are teaching me to forgive others.

Hallelujah! I praise you for your power!

You sought out the desolate, burned-out shell in which I huddled, nursing my grudges. You entered willingly, offering to replace the acrid stench of my resentment with life; you brought freshness, sweetness, growth.

Hallelujah! I thank you for your love!

You alone, Lord, bring life and hope! You alone set my heart free through the miracle of forgiveness—both to me and through me.

It works! Whoopee!

You alone produce wholeness and meaning, which are available to me, to all of us, through the sacrifice of Jesus, in whose name I pray. Amen.

9. Pray for healing. There are two kinds of emotional healing for which we can pray. We may pray that the memories of the incident will no longer be painful. Or we may pray that God will fill the emptiness caused by the absence of a normal and necessary relationship, such as a child growing up without one or both parents, or by the absence of closeness in a relationship, such as a child growing up without any emotional closeness to a parent.

10. Keep the issue closed. Refuse to think about it any more. The discipline of praying in thanksgiving can be helpful here. And serving others is a very positive and valuable way to release our minds from thoughts of past or present difficulties.

Some people have thought about an old grievance so much that it is necessary for them to use a systematic method to retrain their thought patterns. Here is a method that is useful in such situations. When the unwanted thought intrudes, say the word "Stop!" We may say it either out loud or to ourselves, but we must say it with authority and then turn our thinking to something else—even something meaningless like counting or reciting the alphabet. Or make the exercise more challenging by counting backward from 387 by 7's or by reciting the alphabet backward. Better yet, recite a Scripture verse, pray with thanksgiving, or count your blessings. Any of these activities will displace the unwanted thought with something neutral or positive.

This method is most useful in situations when the unwanted thought has been a frequent intruder over several months or more. It encourages us to take individual responsibility for our mental acts and can be a wholesome way of participating in the process of renewing our minds (Rom. 12:2).

11. Use assertive behavior to minimize future hurt. We are to exercise stewardship over our emotional lives as well as over our physical selves and other resources. It is wrong for us to go looking for trouble or to make it easy for others to abuse us because this reduces our capacity to praise and serve God and makes us a party to the other person's wrong behavior.

The action plan form on the next page is designed to help us identify those we need to forgive. Make as many copies of it as you need so you will have one for each person you need to forgive. Remember once again that this is not a rigid process and that I am not suggesting a legalistic formula, but rather, a way of systematically opening ourselves to God's direction on these matters and prompting ourselves to resolve them. Pray before working on these.

We must commit ourselves to knowing God's truth and using that truth, no matter how painful it might be. Following God's truth always leads to a good place.

MY ACTION PLAN FOR FORGIVING _____ (initials of the person I need to forgive)

In the space provided below, list the injustices for which you need to forgive this person. In the "Present Status" column, use the appropriate code numbers from the list that follows. Then list the ways you have responded to this person in the past, using an asterisk to indicate those responses for which you need to apologize; what you should do next; and the date by which you will do it.

Injustices I need to forgive:

	Present Status
_____	_____
_____	_____
_____	_____

    0 I still have resentment and a desire to retaliate.
    1 I am out of fellowship with God because I have not forgiven.
    2 I have quit hurting the other person.
    3 I am willing to want to apologize and forgive.
    4 I want to apologize and forgive.
    5 I am trying to determine if I should talk with the person.
    6 I have apologized and am making restitution.
    7 I have forgiven the person.
    8 I am claiming the forgiving and the forgiveness.
    9 I am praying that my memories will be healed.
  10 I am working on keeping the issue closed.
  11 I am learning assertive behavior to minimize future hurt.

P—Add a "P" in front of the number if you are praying about the situation the number represents.

T—Add a "T" in front of the number if you are talking with a reliable friend about it.

Ways I have responded in the past and those responses for which I need to apologize:

_____
_____
_____

What I should do next:

	Target Date
_____	_____
_____	_____
_____	_____

17 | Living the Forgiving:
The Forgiver's Lifestyle

WE ARE NEVER FAR from the need to forgive. Until Christ returns, this world will remain broken and sinful, and people will continue to hurt one another, thus creating the need for forgiveness.

Forgiving does not change the other person or protect us from more hurt. Forgiving changes us. It creates in us an attitude of compassion and understanding, or at least a desire for compassion and understanding. But if we do not forgive, our attitude will produce continuing resentment, the temptation to retaliate, bitterness, and self-pity.

Forgiving also changes our actions. It creates in us a desire to exhibit more loving behavior toward that person, to communicate better, and to learn about any loose ends or additional problems in the relationship. But if we do not forgive, we will continue to try to avoid that person and to retaliate directly or indirectly.

Often we may remain involved in the life of the person we have forgiven. We may be with the person a lot or we may have only an invisible, emotional tie—but either way we should seek appropriate ways to express God's grace and mercy to him or her. Paul says it all in Romans 12:17–21, "Do not repay anyone evil for evil.

Be careful to do what is right in the eyes of everybody. If it is possible, as far as it depends on you, live at peace with everyone. Do not take revenge, my friends, but leave room for God's wrath, for it is written: 'It is mine to avenge; I will repay,' says the Lord. On the contrary: 'If your enemy is hungry, feed him; if he is thirsty, give him something to drink. In doing this, you will heap burning coals on his head.' Do not be overcome by evil, but overcome evil with good."

This indicates that we are God's representative to the person who has hurt us—a big responsibility. But fortunately, God has not only appointed us to be His representatives, He has promised us the strength to represent Him effectively!

To do this we must pray for wisdom and patience and be obedient to God's counsel; for obedience always leads ultimately to joy, even though the path may go through painful, dangerous terrain. Then we will discover God's eagerness to go with us through the hard times and His never-ending desire to help us emerge victorious. This will give us new freedom and greater wholeness and enable us to pray with thanksgiving for God's healing and for His presence within us.

> Thank you, Lord, for helping me forgive. Help me to humbly know, always, that it is not by my power but by yours that I have been able to let go of the resentment I have felt. Keep me vigilant for my tendency to be vindictive and petty. Let there be no condescension—no looking down my nose— toward the person I've forgiven.
>
> You love me, and you ask me to love others in the same way. That assignment overwhelms me, but then, your love overwhelms me, too. Allow me to bask in your love so I may develop the capacity—determination, honesty, unselfishness —to love those around me fully and anonymously.
>
> I praise you and pray this in the name of your holy Son, Jesus, Amen.